CHASING THE
MORNING SUN

Flying solo round the world in a homebuilt aircraft:
the ultimate adventure

Manuel Queiroz

Grub Street · London

Published by
Grub Street
4 Rainham Close
London
SW11 6SS

British Library Cataloguing in Publication Data
Queiroz, Manuel.
   Chasing the morning sun : flying solo round the world in a
   homebuilt aircraft - the ultimate adventure.
   1. Queiroz, Manuel. 2. Flights around the world.
   3. Airplanes, Home-built. 4. Air pilots—Great Britain—
   Biography.
   I. Title
   629.1'3'092-dc22

ISBN-13: 9781908117090

Cover design by Sarah Driver
Edited by Sophie Campbell
Formatted by Sarah Driver
Maps by Jon Paull
Chasing the Morning Sun logo by Ben Ashman

Printed and bound by MPG Ltd, Bodmin, Cornwall

Grub Street Publishing only uses
FSC (Forest Stewardship Council) paper for its books.

CONTENTS

Foreword

A round the world flight is never something to be undertaken lightly, especially flying solo. Good preparation is the key and attention to detail is imperative. However, as you will read in the following pages even the best made plans can be disrupted. The weather is the main factor, with the overriding question being, 'is it safe to fly in any given weather?' The round the world pilot is forever facing bureaucratic challenges with every country having its own quirks and demands. Despite faith in his flying machine, the solo pilot must check and recheck the condition and performance of the aircraft.

Written in a modest, and sometimes self effacing way, Manuel Queiroz tells of the difficulties and dangers of undertaking a solo world flight in a tiny aircraft. We explore with Manuel the meticulous preparations and then see them dashed to pieces when things don't go the way that is planned. We feel the frustrations when the fuel that was promised isn't there and we share the necessity to control anger as bureaucracy rears its head to obstruct progress.

What is so amazing is that this flight, which took only thirty-nine days to cover 23,527nm, was organised by one man and a wonderfully supportive wife. The determination along with huge amounts of courage is an inspiration to us all. It was more the norm to fly for ten hours day after day with sometimes little or no rest in between and on top of this Manuel was fighting a lingering bronchitis. This challenge was definitely not for the faint hearted.

Manuel shares with us his innermost feelings throughout the flight. His spirits soar to enormous heights as he marvels at the wonders of this world from 10,000ft above the ground, and he muses, rightly, on the power of such things as tsunamis and volcanoes making him realise how small we all are in the big scheme of things. He also conveys the disappointment and depression that sets in when humans display suffering at the abuse of others.

Overcoming fear of the unknown is at the heart of this story. In Manuel's own words, 'courage is having fear and finding a way to overcome it'. Fear certainly reared its ugly head when taking off in the dark for the longest leg in the world from Hilo in Hawaii to San Jose in California. This was a distance of 2,016nm over shark-infested Pacific waters with very little chance of being found in a tiny life raft if things had gone wrong.

The one thing that stands out is that wherever Manuel landed there was someone there to help, and to befriend him. This support from ordinary people from every race and culture who were prepared to put themselves out without asking for anything in return is what really underpins this whole story.

This is a spiritual journey as well as a challenge that demands enormous focus. Above all, I feel this is a love story and this reaches to the very core of us all.

Polly Vacher
April 2011

Introduction
A DISTANT DREAM

"I am going to fly solo around the world!"

I made this theatrical announcement in November 2000 aboard a ship off Cape Horn, that most notorious and fearsome nautical landmark. Sailing past that lonely and weathered piece of land was an extraordinary experience that I found both spiritually challenging and inspirational. Its very presence gave me the push that was needed to turn long-held aspirations into a process that culminated in my solo around the world flight.

Admittedly, this announcement was not my most thought-out decision – in fact it was borne from a lot of enthusiastic talk and bravado within a group of half a dozen people trying to find ways of surpassing the experiences and dramatic plans of each other. Such a flamboyant gesture was rewarded by suitably admiring gasps perfectly serving my dramatic aspirations of the time and giving me the top spot for daring plans. The delayed dark side of my announcement hit me later on in the confines of my cabin as I started to realise the enormity of the task I had talked myself into. Little did I know just how huge it really was going to be.

Turning the clock back a few years, I had started flying in 1990 following a chance encounter with the, then, relatively new microlight machines. The desire to fly, repressed over many years by the usual family and financial pressures, was at last allowed to flourish and I was able to discover the sense of freedom known only to those who have 'slipped the surly bonds of earth'.

I found flying full of previously unimaginable delights. One of its most outstanding aspects was the ability to see what nature normally hides from us ground-hugging, wingless creatures. The very act of flying a small aircraft allows a view of the world that is not only vastly superior to the keyhole glimpse allowed by the average airliner window, but it is much more than just a view – it is an introduction to a new world. It is not simply passive either – the wonder of flight gives us the opportunity to search for fantastic new experiences guided by our own free will. As the icing on the cake, this search is conducted in a glorious and previously unreachable three-dimensional freedom; high above all the paths to which earth-bound creatures are confined.

By apparently severing the connection between ourselves and Mother Earth, we actually gain an intimate bond with our planet – an astonishing achievement, especially as this experience is not simply limited to better knowing its surface. We also become intimate with the atmosphere within which we move, complete with all the complexities and secrets that are hidden from those who haven't experienced the exhilaration of flight. We simply must experience navigating within that invisible wonder we call the atmosphere to fully love, admire and respect all its beauty and power – no description of mine will ever do it justice.

In my progression through the world of aviation every flight brought new discoveries, every discovery fuelled the need for wider frontiers and eventually I felt I needed to conquer the ultimate flight. I had to fly around the world…

I began to replace microlights with more conventional machinery, if a Jodel aeroplane can be described this way. This didn't change the core of the experience; it just offered a slightly different perspective.

Moving forward to 1999, fate had in store a surprise that was going to greatly influence all my thinking. During what should have been a routine appendicectomy, my alert surgeon discovered and removed a cancer of the colon. This was a cancer at a very early stage, so much so that I was not aware of any symptoms and I was declared cured within a very short space of time. Previously, of course, I had always thought these things only happened to others and couldn't possibly have happened to me. But it had.

I was suddenly very aware of my own mortality. Such an event rearranges life priorities, and what to fit into one's time on this planet is then seen in a very different light. Time was no longer endless; life really has to take into account its own finite nature.

So standing on the deck of that ship off Cape Horn I really did reach the decision to fly around the world, those words weren't just empty rhetoric. The thought of venturing above all the continents and flying high above the oceans in order to undertake the longest journey on earth did have a terrific appeal for the navigator within me. The journey that takes in all the climates, above all landscapes and comes into contact with mankind from all backgrounds, races and creeds was an opportunity that the romantic in me could not ignore. The challenge to overcome the extremes of weather; the most isolated parts of the world's deserts and oceans; the hectic airspace of the great hubs of population; the taming of a small flying machine that is being extended beyond its design parameters: all this was an irresistible challenge for the pilot in me.

There was another element much more difficult to quantify and rationalise: this came from a thirst for knowledge, the wish to discover what lies beneath the obvious. How much could I discover about the world? Could I further my perception of nature? What was I going to find that I hadn't even anticipated?

It is often said that having a dream is easy but making it a reality is quite a distinct and much more difficult matter. Whilst this could appear to be the case, I believe that such a statement is a huge oversimplification; maybe even the opposite is true. Having a dream that is worth pursuing can help overcome the grind of daily life. But actually daring to take hold of this dream in all its glory is the really difficult part. Turning the dream into reality is easier because you have a clear and illuminated purpose.

Obviously, the difficulties of overcoming practical obstacles in realising an ambitious dream are and remain very real, but I firmly believe that the motivation from our inspiration is the strongest force to overcome all barriers on the way to our chosen goal.

It was time for me to face those obstacles. Many thoughts and considerations about all manner of practical problems kept invading my mind in waves, seldom well defined, but always with a tremendous impact. In 2001 I realised it was time to form a structured and realistic plan.

Of course none of this could have happened without the support of my wife Jill. I know that without outside help, it takes more determination and dedication than I can possibly muster for such an undertaking. Not that I had ever before committed myself to such an enormous project. Jill had deep misgivings about the whole concept and, as a former pilot in her own right, was especially aware of the dangers involved, such as the limitations of a small aircraft and my own limitations as a private pilot. Up to that point my longest flight had only lasted some four hours, and my longest single sea crossing covered fifty nautical miles (92km). I was now planning to fly seventeen hours at a time, while crossing over 2,000 nautical miles (3,700km) of ocean. There were also the ever-present financial considerations. Unless a high-level sponsorship was to be found, the huge and essential financial commitment would have left her in a particularly vulnerable position if it had all gone wrong.

Jill's monumentally unselfish support for my dream-chasing is an outstanding display of a generous, altruistic and self-sacrificing spirit for the sole purpose of supporting her singularly lucky and foolish husband.

THE IDEA TAKING FORM

The research required for the task ahead was an incredible eye-opener. The world, despite the popular saying to the contrary, is decidedly not small. As the vast majority of the planet's surface is water and the seasons of the year are completely different from one place to another, the right timing of favourable weather patterns for a continuous rapid journey around the globe has to be the result of a very fine balancing act. As well as finding a way around these natural problems, I also had to consider the legal requirements of many countries and the legendary difficulties accessing the authorities that control the use of their airspace. It soon became obvious that the task ahead was going to be monumental.

And the essential element missing for a round the world flight was, of course, an aeroplane! So, finding a suitable aircraft seemed a good starting point. While evaluating types of aircraft and the combination of elements that could make it all happen, I thought that trying to attempt some world records (might as well aim for the top) constituted a neat way of gathering the project together and giving direction to my ambitions. Looking through the list of possible official world records, I felt I wanted to try for a record that would favour an attempt by a solo pilot and trying for a speed record for the whole circumnavigation of the globe was an obvious choice all around. I also felt that such a record attempt would help to shape the structure of the project.

All aeronautical competitions and records are overseen by an official international organisation, the Fédération Aéronautique Internationale (FAI). It has its headquarters in Switzerland and regulates all forms of air sports in the world. The FAI is usually represented in the individual countries by their national aero club, which in the case of the UK is the Royal Aero Club (RAeC). The governing regulations of the FAI are contained in a document entitled the 'sporting code', the study of which was the starting point of a long and steep learning curve.

One of the first things to learn was that in order to be considered as a valid record claim, a circumnavigation flight needs to comply with a number of requirements. A journey that does not comply with all the specific regulations simply wouldn't qualify, irrespective of the achieved performance. Amongst these requirements: the individually chosen route must be pre-approved, must start and finish at the same aerodrome, cross all meridians in the same direction outside the Arctic or Antarctic zones, cover no less than 20,943.6nm/ 36,787.559km (the length of the Tropic of Cancer) and all the elapsed time counts towards the average speed calculations. In other words, all time not actually travelling still counts towards the total, so time spent on the ground must be kept to a minimum.

With apologies to all navigators reading these lines, this is nevertheless a convenient time to look at a few definitions. The nautical mile, so often mentioned in these pages, is a long-established and convenient way of measuring distances over long journeys, the type of journey navigated by ships and later by aeroplanes. A nautical mile is defined as the distance covered by a minute ($\frac{1}{60}$th of a degree) of latitude.[1] The relation of the nautical mile to the dimensions of the earth conveniently allows measurements on a chart by comparing the actual distance to be measured with the latitude markings, easily achieved with a set of dividers. A nautical mile is equivalent to 1.15 statute miles. The related measure of speed is the nautical mile per hour and is known as the knot. The distances between any two points for FAI record purposes are always measured as great circle (GC) distances. A GC distance is the shortest distance between two points along the surface of the globe, it could be said that it is the equivalent of a straight line on flat surface![2]

The technicalities of the FAI requirements, although possibly not the most scintillating topic, defined the choice of aircraft type for the task ahead. Reading the FAI sporting code, it was soon clear that too large or too small an aeroplane would have critical disadvantages for what I was envisaging. The possibility of using too small an aeroplane with a limited range would have necessitated a choice of route following the rim of the Pacific, and include an inevitable crossing of the airspace of Russia and China and/or visiting the Aleutian Isles. Any one of these choices would have been potentially disastrous for a speed record. The eastern parts of these two Asian countries had a dreadful reputation for creating unreasonable bureaucratic demands, usually resulting in unjustifiable delays for flights complying with visual flight rules (VFR). And the Aleutians probably have the most unpredictable weather anywhere on the planet.

Visual flight rules are a set of regulations which allow a pilot to operate an aircraft in weather conditions generally clear enough so the pilot can see where the aircraft is going. This was the kind of flight I envisaged carrying out, where I would rely on visual reference to the outside. The weather must be better than basic VFR weather minimums, as specified in the rules of the relevant aviation authority. If the weather is worse, pilots are required to use instrument flight rules (IFR), where flights rely on the ability of being solely conducted by reference to the appropriate instruments. VFR requires a pilot to be able to see outside the cockpit, to control the aircraft's attitude, navigate, and avoid obstacles and other aircraft.

IFR permits an aircraft to operate in instrument meteorological conditions (IMC), which have much lower weather minimums than VFR. IMC exists when visual reference to the outside is lost and the pilot requires appropriate instruments and training to successfully fly with sole reference to navigational instruments.

To use too large an aircraft would be attempting to break records already set by multiple crews that can accommodate rest periods for individual pilots without the need to interrupt the journey, not to mention the bigger budgets that are associated with the larger aircraft.

Based on these considerations, the choice of aircraft had to be in-between those extremes and I settled for class C1-B of the FAI, the class concerned with landplanes of a maximum take-off weight (MTOW) between 500kg and 1,000kg. This includes many basic two-seater trainers and the majority of the so-called experimental aeroplanes. The former are invariably solid and staid machines that are certified to international standards which comply with strict manufacturing rules, provenance standards and rigid maintenance schedules.[3] However they are also of predictable and consistent behaviour and will look after pilots of varying abilities and experience. The latter are more difficult to define as there is no international certification aspect and therefore many versions of these 'experimental' aircraft definitions are in existence. Being independent of the constraints of international standards, they can sometimes be endowed with qualities that that cannot be certified for a variety of reasons. This freedom gives inventive individuals and small forward-thinking companies the possibility to create a very high-performance aircraft. However the performance might have to be balanced by greater demands on the pilot's workload and an inconsistent level of quality control, both at the building and maintenance stages.

The existing circumnavigation record in class C1-B was established in 2000 by a very successful and enormously-experienced pilot, the late Hans G Schmid of Switzerland in his home-built 'LongEz', a very unusual-looking high-performance composite aircraft. The combination of the LongEz's performance and Hans Schmid's ability set a very difficult record to beat – although I felt it might just be possible to break. A great challenge loomed ahead.

My choice of aircraft to chase Schmid's record would have to come from the experimental arena if there was going to be a possibility of improving on his splendid performance. From the possible options, I narrowed the choice down to the current record holder, the LongEz, and the more conventional Van's RV range of aircraft, one of which was the previous holder of the same record.

These two aircraft types, as long-distance contenders, have a very similar performance in the air, but achieve that by very different means. In fact they have completely opposing design philosophies and construction methods. Their similarities are confined to both aircraft being of homebuilt construction and regrettably suffering from an incredibly long construction time, typically over 2,000 man hours. This made the decision to buy an already constructed aeroplane very easy. My own lack of knowledge of composite construction (plastics, fibreglass and similar) and the inherent difficulty of inspecting the completed work favoured the RV solution with its conventional all-metal structure. The shorter take-off run of the RV and its less quirky handling clinched it.

Although chasing the world speed record was important and gave the project its skeleton, it was of secondary importance to the actual circumnavigation. A possible world record would have been the icing on the cake, but certainly not the cake! The biggest motivation was, after all, to actually complete the journey all the way around the world and become one of only sixty solo pilots in the whole of aviation history to have ever completed it in a single-engined aircraft. Other important goals were to attempt to be the first British pilot to complete such a flight in this aircraft class, the first in a British-registered homebuilt aircraft and one of only six pilots of any nationality to have ever completed a circumnavigation flight in a homebuilt aircraft.

At a different level, the research of possible routes and all the attendant problems started during a period of great change in the general process of acquiring information. Throughout the time I spent preparing for the big trip, I had the opportunity to witness the extraordinarily rapid expansion of the internet and its practical everyday use. What is now taken for granted in terms of gathering data from around the world about any subject, would not so long ago have been a painfully slow and frustrating process. Enquiring 'cold' about such vital things as fuel availability in remote places was at times a monumental task, no doubt made even more difficult by my not being personally connected with the air transport industry. It has been fascinating to experience the development of the internet as a phenomenally powerful tool.

2001 was a year of research at an unhurried pace and this was the first sign of a massive underestimation of the task ahead. The year drifted by looking for a suitable aircraft and trying to piece together a sensible route, but not achieving a great deal in terms of actual progress. During the Christmas holiday of that year it became obvious that a timetable was going to be needed.

The end of 2001 was a major landmark in the development of the project as various significant aspects were started at that time: an actual 'to do' list with a timetable (admittedly to be changed many times afterwards); the decision to support the charity Cancer Research UK; and a business program to generate the essential sponsorship. At the same time it was decided that the ideal time for the flight to take place would be sometime in 2003. The particular reason for this was a personal celebration of the centenary of powered aviation and it seemed appropriate to dedicate the spirit of adventure of this flight to the pioneering attitude of the Wright brothers. Planning so far ahead obviously had the advantage of ensuring that this project would avoid last-minute rushes and panics as I had a lot of spare time on my hands. Time itself was going to show I still had an awful lot to learn about schedules!

Anticipating the multiple difficulties of piloting over such enormous distances, it was decided that an instrument qualification and a night rating were going to be essential additions to my pilot licence, irrespective of the legal aspects of flying this type of aircraft away from day visual flight rules. Over the distances I was contemplating, relying on the weather to allow VFR conditions all of the time, with no exceptions whatsoever, would have been exceedingly optimistic. The most common cause of fatal accidents in light aircraft is leaving 'visual conditions' and entering instrument meteorological conditions without the correct training. To avoid this, I undertook an IMC course and gained the appropriate rating on my licence in the summer of 2002. A night rating was also achieved at around the same time.

As business was leaving little time for the necessary chasing of potential sponsors, I 'volunteered' my good friend Graham Shimmin for the job of project manager. He sportingly agreed to take on the role for free.

Graham came up with a most impressive list of potential sponsors, a bit of a who's who, really. We immediately learnt the hard way the difficulties in gaining a substantial sponsorship: you need a proven track record, to get a proven record you need lots of money of your own or, well…er, sponsorship! It is a vicious circle and it requires a frightening amount of determination to persevere. From my days of competing with motor cars, I knew the path to sponsorship to be an arduous one; now that the goals were much bigger, the path was steeper and more hostile than ever. Anybody contemplating this route simply cannot accept defeat when refusals come in from all directions at a horrific rate and keep on coming. The alternative to being bombarded with refusals is to be completely ignored, which feels no better. This was decidedly not for the faint hearted.

To keep the goal in sight and to maintain a positive attitude, I found that the inspiration derived from two special individuals helped me enormously through all these tribulations. One is somebody I have never had the good fortune to meet: Ellen MacArthur. Now Dame Ellen, she is an inspiration to anybody that wants to pursue their dreams. Her total dedication to her cause is simply second to none and much as I am inspired by her deeds, I don't think I am either made of the same strong stuff as her or young enough to have her complete commitment, but I tried. The other great influence came from Polly Vacher, the twice around the world aviatrix. Her generosity with advice was only matched by her thoroughness in preparation and planning. Apart from her technical advice about this type of flying, she gave me one maxim that has stayed with me ever since: "Get advice from many sources, but make the decisions yourself." This helped me immensely on a number of important occasions.

It was interesting to note that these influences, as well as the inspiration from my own wife Jill, were all from women. There are clearly a much greater number of male adventurers than female but I came to the conclusion that, unlike men, their thinking is not tainted by vast amounts of testosterone, the hormone which must be the most effective antidote to reason. My past experience seems to confirm this.

Throughout 2002 I spent a significant amount of time looking through the various publications with aircraft for sale both in the UK and in North America. The disparity of specifications and prices for very similar descriptions were at best confusing and, short of investing a lot of time and money travelling around both sides of the Atlantic, not very easy to process.

In October 2002 a classified advert in an aviation magazine led me to a Van's RV-6 on a Yorkshire airstrip. This was a low-time aircraft that had been built in Canada, it was registered G-GDRV and, with its relatively simple construction and specification, did appear to be well-suited to the task. The necessary financial undertaking to raise the required capital was the start of a really serious commitment.

Chapter 1
THE DREAM TAKES SHAPE:
THE ENGINEERING PROCESS

As expected, the arrival of G-GDRV constituted a major turning point of the project.

It was delivered to me at Gloucestershire airport, Staverton by the previous owner on 12th December 2002. While returning the previous owner by road to his home in Yorkshire, disaster struck when a good deed from a friend went wrong. As my friend opened the canopy to put the aeroplane to bed in a hangar, a gust of wind overcame the inadequate canopy stay and caused a substantial amount of damage. This was especially annoying as I hadn't even sat in the aircraft, let alone flown it. The following day I tried my hardest to discount this episode as a bad omen for the project and convinced myself that this was just a lesson in overcoming disappointment. Little did I know just how many times this sort of lesson was to occur along the way.

Once a temporary repair was carried out to the canopy and surrounding area, the ensuing period learning about the aircraft was particularly pleasant and it certainly was a most exciting time. The fabulous performance of G-GDRV (or G-RV for short) compared with all the other aircraft I had previously flown was just mind-blowing, the equivalent of driving a Ferrari versus utilitarian Fiats. Discovering this level of performance was also a learning process about my capabilities as a pilot. The only slightly disturbing characteristic I was to discover (and make me temporarily lose composure) was a dramatic left-wing drop at the stall, making the aircraft snap an instant 90° roll to the left.[4] At the time I accepted (or convinced myself) that this wing drop was a possible behaviour trait of this type of aircraft. Much was to be found out about this issue later.

Evaluating the aeroplane's potential for the round the world flight was often delayed by the sheer pleasure of 'boring holes in the sky'. That, in itself, wasn't quite as much a waste of time as it might sound because it helped me to get to know the aircraft intimately. This knowledge was going to be invaluable to determine what I required to execute my ambitious flight.

The beginning of 2003 started in an optimistic mood and the whole idea felt much more feasible and real. Having an aeroplane to carry out the flight helped a great deal, and led to a more positive attitude towards approaching potential sponsors with a credible plan and generally re-invigorating the project.

At around that time, my good friend Ben Ashman (of microlight, hang glider and aviation artistry fame), came up with the perfect title for the project, which was of course, 'Chasing the Morning Sun', and my much-loved logo. With this inspirational title and drawing Ben had perfectly encapsulated the spirit of the project. First of all the graphic image had the immediately obvious image of the RV flying towards the east; for me it carried an allegorical reference to the dawn of an era when cancer might join the ranks of other tamed diseases. It had the romantic beauty and aesthetic inspiration to go towards the source of all energy and of course, it had the splendid contradictory element of chasing something that cannot be caught.

These were positive aspects that made the project feel realistic, achievable and charged with energy. There were also times when the path towards my goal didn't feel so achievable, such as when two separate and apparently enthusiastic potential sponsors either had a hidden agenda or were expecting instant gratification for no investment on their part. The offer of a website service that came to nothing but outrageous claims without actually providing anything was one example. The other was the offer from Wolverhampton airport as a place of preparation and headquarters for the flight. Once the media interest went away after the press launch and the hard slog of the preparation started, the management of the time replaced their offer by a removal ultimatum at short notice, with complete disregard for the hardship and logistical nightmare they caused. By then the aircraft was sufficiently stripped to be unable to fly out and only the help of a number of friends made its transportation by road possible in the available time.

The solution was to take the aircraft into my workshops in Halesowen, West Midlands, where the bulk of the preparation work took place. The only possible way that the aircraft was going to be prepared for this flight was by carrying out the work myself – the hoped for 'big sponsor' never materialised, therefore the subsequent financial situation wasn't going to allow for the hire of expensive resources. Fortunately I was in a position to do this myself. My engineering background and many years in the restoration and preparation of competition and classic cars gave me the necessary skills to carry out that work, from the planning through to the execution of all the modifications and improvements. The generous help of a few friends was invaluable and I will be forever grateful to all of you guys.

The website fiasco was resolved by Jill setting up our own site, at first as a temporary solution and then by developing it into the working solution that it finally became. Jill is not an IT professional so this was a brave and generous action that resulted in a most fitting site, a further example of her invaluable support.

One of the difficulties of undertaking the massive preparation for the round the world flight is that when you are simultaneously the head designer, engineer and floor sweeper, time decreases with the number of tasks being undertaken. It finally dawned on me that it was already 2003 and the possibility of carrying out the flight to celebrate the century of powered flight just wasn't going to happen.

Adding to that frustration, one of the more ridiculous episodes during that period took place around the spring of that year while trying to acquire global meteorological information. To establish where and when I could attempt my flight, such information was critical for the planning of the route. Having always been interested in travelling, I had a reasonable idea of the climates around the world, but I needed much more than a fair notion before committing myself to such an undertaking.

My first and most obvious port of call was the UK's Met Office, then based in Bracknell. The reaction I had from that office was somewhat startling; they told me that the only type of data I could hope for was going to be historic as no forecasts would be possible over the sort of time span I was contemplating. A part of me thought this probably was the only sensible thing they ever said in view of their success rate for short-term forecasts. I now appreciate that my frustration caused an unbalanced bias and I have since learnt that a forecast can't extend to that length of time, so historic climatological data would have to do. However, to actually acquire that data from them was something else. After several enquiries I was informed that such a service would cost, "something in the region of £500", with which I agreed, despite finding it exorbitantly expensive. This, it has to be remembered, was for old and straightforward data, not for a forecast. Having accepted these costs and despite multiple reminders, I still did not actually receive anything, not even an invoice.

Several complaints over many weeks (including one to the 'top man') and I finally gave up on the British Meteorological Office. For a service that is charged with supporting aviation, I found the whole system greatly inadequate. In marked contrast, the staff of Meteo France office in Toulouse, my next port of call, were most professional, courteous and prompt in satisfying my request. They charged me, but they delivered.

As time was passing quickly, it seemed appropriate to replace the link to the aviation century's celebrations with the project's expressed support for the fight against cancer. I decided to name the aircraft SLAVKA in memory of a dear friend who had lost her battle against cancer, a battle that was fought around the same time as my own skirmish. It was felt that her much missed and larger than life presence could be celebrated by taking her name to the skies of the world in a suitably-flamboyant style.

In the practical world of finding funds, the efforts to gather sponsorship were rewarded by gaining the support of E H Smith Ltd, Eastgate and Swaine Adeney Brigg. The generosity of these companies not only made a significant difference to the finances of the project, but also greatly boosted morale.

With the new confidence derived from this support, I decided to attend a high-profile public event in 2003 and try to drum up as much support and sponsorship as possible. The obvious occasion was the Popular Flying Association (PFA) Rally in Kemble during July, complete with the hire of an exhibition stand to maximise impact. The PFA Rally was the greatest celebration of private flying in the world outside the USA and in that year it had arrivals in the region of 2,000 aeroplanes in one weekend. This is a staggering figure that made the airspace around Kemble in the Cotswolds the busiest airspace in the world for the duration of the event. It was clearly a golden opportunity to publicise the flight.

During the preparation for the PFA Rally I experienced a further negative reaction, this time from Cancer Research UK. I was barred from using their logo because I wasn't able to forecast how much money I was going to raise for their charity. At one point I actually contemplated changing my support to another cancer charity, but because I firmly believed in their work, I carried on without their logo which, to this day, I still have not been authorised to use.

The 'Chasing the Morning Sun' stand at the PFA Rally enjoyed great and virtually universal support. It was also at this event that one of the project's most successful fundraising operations was started, giving supporting individuals the opportunity to have their name written on the wings of the aircraft. This allowed the names of these supporters to be flown on G-RV around the world in exchange for a donation upwards of £20 – there was no upper limit, of course! Such a simple idea proved to be very popular and was also going to lend tremendous moral support to me as every time and anywhere in the world I was to look at my wings I could see the names of those that were actually supporting me, making me feel a lot less isolated in my endeavours.

In addition to this success, an unexpected amount of practical advice was received from people carrying out long-distance flights. CarolAnn Garrett, an American pilot stopping over in Kemble during her solo flight around the world in her Mooney aircraft, with just the Atlantic to cross before the completion of her full circumnavigation, was a mine of information. With her totally up to the minute experience, she did point out a number of facts that weren't obvious to me, demonstrating that the camaraderie amongst long-distance pilots and particularly round the world flyers (accomplished or to be accomplished) is amazingly strong. Not to mention this group being be the most reliable and greatest source of 'real facts'. Bill Harrelson and his wife had crossed the Atlantic from their native Florida in a homebuilt Lancair just to attend the PFA Rally and he too was most generous with his advice. Being able to draw from their experience was a tremendously valuable opportunity.

On a not so positive note, no new companies joined the sponsorship list. However, weighing that against the positive reception, advice received and the wing name scheme, the balance was decidedly favourable, a worthwhile move.

THE ENGINEERING PROCESS

Despite hopes to the contrary, it wasn't long before I discovered that preparing the aircraft for this task involved about the same amount of work as building the whole thing from scratch. To cheer myself I kept saying that if I started with something in working order it should still be so afterwards...

This was my initial working list to prepare the aircraft:

- Strip all covers and sub-assemblies for thorough inspection of airframe
- Make good all found faults
- Install new electric equipment to meet the planned demands
- Have the engine fully overhauled and all updates carried out
- Discard existing inadequate instrument panel
- Design and build a new instrument panel with all navigation, radio and monitoring equipment required for this flight
- Incorporate modifications to ensure reliability and ease of use
- Design and install additional fuel tanks to triple the endurance
- Modify the airframe to carry the extra weight of fuel and maintain the centre of gravity within its limits.

Starting the rebuild and, *right*, a very bare panel

The construction craftsmanship of the airframe appeared good and it adhered to sound principles, which was reassuring. It also became apparent that it had been built within a tight budget, resulting in a simplicity that was an actual advantage for the task ahead. However, the fuel tanks were the only exceptions to the good build quality as a sealant commonly known as 'sloshing compound' was flaking inside the tanks and threatening to block the fuel lines, with the very real possibility of causing an unexpected engine stoppage. After a lot of hard work the sealant was removed, making me wonder why is it so difficult to deliberately get rid of something that seems to simply fall off when left alone.

Although the actual build workmanship was good, a number of adjustments made previously were very poor. The most obvious one was the movement range of the aerodynamic controls, as this was actually dangerous. How these serious mistakes passed the necessary inspections for airworthiness both in Canada and in the UK is a mystery to me. Fortunately, the corrections of these faults were quite straightforward and were some of the easiest tasks of the whole project.

The electric system was one of the worst I have ever seen and the only solution was to throw it all away and start again. This allowed me to commence with a clean sheet to redesign the whole set-up and integrate it with a newly self-designed instrument panel to make the best use of the limited space. I used switches that are also circuit breakers to make it as light and simple as possible.

> *Why is aircraft electric wire white?* The wires used in cars have a coloured PVC insulation for ease of identification. In a fire this PVC gives off poisonous fumes and, as the immediate evacuation of an airborne aircraft is seldom possible, we don't use them. The colour identification might have been useful despite being limited by the number of colours, but as in very large wiring looms this would also be ineffective. It is considered preferable to eliminate colour altogether.

The new instrument panel was built around a GPS Skymap IIIC, my preferred navigational tool for the task ahead. I found this unit very user-friendly with a moving colour map and great capabilities for VFR flight, a reasonable IFR database and easy to install data cartridges for various parts of the world. Along with the GPS, Bendix-King helped me with a generous deal for the combined navigation and communication very high frequency (VHF) radio set. This came complete with a course deviation indicator (CDI) to allow the use of instrument landing systems (ILS) and a transponder with altitude reporting capability (mode 'C'). The avionics were completed by a two-axis TruTrak autopilot, a fantastic piece of kit that came with a good discount from its manufacturers. Finally I had an Icom ham radio set modified to work in the aviation HF frequencies for the long sea crossings. The illumination of the panel and cockpit made use of instrument 'P' lights and some ingenious swivelling map and cabin lamps. The flight instruments were positioned in a slightly modified version of the conventional six dial set up, with the air speed indicator (ASI)

The kitchen table – where new instrument panels start!

replaced by a new instrument allowing a direct reading of true air speed (TAS) and taking its pressure from a new heated pitot tube. All of this took up most of the panel space, so the engine instruments and several new additions in the form of fuel management, timers and temperature gauges were all replaced by a compact engine monitor from Rocky Mountains. Electric power came from a 60 amp alternator of automotive origin and a lightweight high-power battery, both standard items from the Van's Aircraft catalogue.

The Lycoming O-320 engine was taken to Ronaldson Aviation for a complete overhaul as the aircraft had been originally built with a time-expired engine and it certainly seemed a good idea to have a fresh one for the ocean crossings ahead.[5] At the same time I reached the decision to up-grade the engine from a 150hp specification to 160hp, not a straightforward exercise. The higher compression of the 160hp version allowed a slightly better thermal efficiency to extend the range but, on the negative side, pretty well excluded the use of car petrol (Mogas/motor gasoline). The possibility of using Mogas, when Avgas (aviation gasoline) is not available could have been a useful option, but ultimately I decided that the extra efficiency outweighed the lack of flexibility.

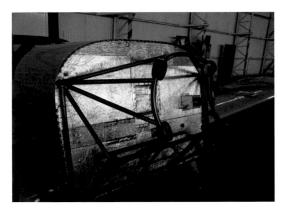 

Engine removed for the rebuild and, *right*, the new shining engine

A new carburettor was fitted with a Van's type airbox, which had a magnetic trap door. This was to avoid impact ice clogging the air intake which would cause engine stoppage, in case I was to stray into conditions that could lead to that predicament. At the same time the engine was fitted with a new standard starter motor, as opposed to a lightweight one, in order to help move the centre of gravity slightly forward. I knew that the original wooden propeller, optimised for climb, would not be able to withstand the erosion of heavy rain in tropical storms, so a different solution had to be found. I chose to install a coarse fixed-pitch metal propeller, which had the added advantage of being more reliable and less expensive than a constant speed one. This would also help to keep the centre of gravity in check as the new metal propeller was considerably heavier than the original.

The biggest departure from standard was going to be the fuel tanks. The good range of the standard RV needed to be improved by a factor of three and finding room for that amount of fuel (and its weight) was going to be a major challenge.

All civil aviation matters in the UK, from microlight to Boeing 747, come under the juris-diction of the Civil Aviation Authority (CAA). The CAA has delegated some of the direct control over the majority of homebuilt aircraft to the Popular Flying Association, later to become the Light Aircraft Association (LAA). The PFA administered the airworthiness of these aircraft con-forming to tightly defined parameters from the CAA. These aircraft were and still are commonly referred to as 'PFA types'. The administration entails checking and approving the design of kits

Starting to try extra fuel tank shapes

or self-designed aircraft that are to be built or used in the UK. This is done by overseeing and inspecting all stages of construction, checking and approving any departures from the original design, both from theoretical and practical considerations and carrying out at least annual inspections to each and every airworthy aircraft that comes under their umbrella. All these actions conform to strictly laid out standards which are not merely guidelines, but are part of the PFA's charter to regulate these aircraft. This is in marked contrast to some other countries where these types of aircraft are much more unregulated and there is little or no attempt to certify them.

These legal considerations were to have a great impact on the whole process of having additional tanks to give the essential huge fuel capacity. If this had been in the USA, I could have made some tanks for whatever capacity and, if weight allowed, that would have been it. In the UK, any fuel tank fitted to these aircraft has to comply with the same standards with which a main fuel tank in a standard aircraft needs to comply with. That means that not only the tank itself has to serve its purpose as a fuel container, but it also needs to demonstrate the construction can withstand extremes of forces in turbulent air, extremes of pressure and sustain a 9 'G' deceleration crash without rupturing.[6] The same goes for the mounting points of these tanks and the fuel system linking them to the airframe and engine.

Perversely, I considered an essential part of the project to have these modifications approved through the British system. The main reason for this was that Britain had become my home country through free choice rather than by the more customary event of being born here. To make the whole project a British venture, as well as any possible reward that might be derived from it, was absolutely essential to me.

Learning the administration system and pushing the project up its steep steps gave rise to many mixed feelings. On the one hand it made me almost despair at the amount of regulation that stifles innovation and loses competitiveness in this sector of aviation. On the other hand it made me even more determined to demonstrate that these goals can be achieved, despite huge difficulties. Thoughts of a nanny state protecting us from ourselves and a past British glory of leadership, now in danger of becoming a fading memory, often depressed me but never affected my determination.

The design and approval of these fuel modifications were invaluably helped by one of my first sponsors, Frazer-Nash Consultancy and the enthusiasm of their marketing manager, Martin Soltau. They specialise in high-profile engineering projects and provide high-tech solutions to industry. Their expertise and help made the difference between succeeding and not. Not that it all went smoothly – one episode that comes to mind was the pressure testing of a wing-tip fuel tank that resulted in it exploding, making me jump more than a little.

Despite valuable help, the process of completing the modifications to the aircraft dragged on through the later part of 2003, all of 2004 and the first half of 2005 – mainly as I was still the only member of staff working on the aircraft. And to make it worse I was not able to dedicate my full attention to the project as I was also trying to run a business as a day job. The other delaying factor involved the PFA as they had to evaluate every step of the process and only had a total of two engineers to look after a fleet of nearly 2,000 aircraft. They clearly were not in a position to dedicate their undivided attention to my project!

When finally completed, the fuel system had a total of six tanks, consisting of the standard main tanks taking 144lt, a pair of tip tanks with a capacity of 68lt, a forward tank in the passenger footwell of 78lt and finally a centre tank (in place of the passenger seat) carrying 160lt. The total capacity of these tanks was therefore 450 litres or 100 imperial/120 US gallons, allowing for a theoretical endurance of up to nineteen hours and a range in still air of 2,400 nautical miles or 4,440km. To carry this extra weight the engine mounting (doubling as the main undercarriage location) was suitably reinforced along the lines of the later Van's RV-7 model. The MTOW was raised from 727kg (1,600lbs) to 907kg (2,000lbs), with a maximum landing weight (MLW) of 818kg (1,800lbs). This new MTOW was only allowed for single occupant use, not that there was any room for a passenger.

The biggest single blow to the preparations happened in December 2004. After refitting the wings and riding on a wave of optimism, I discovered that the port (left) wing was badly twisted. This was devastating news. The twist amounted to three-and-a-half degrees of 'wash-in' which is an unacceptable condition and, despite earlier optimism regarding the original construction, it did put into question the whole build quality.[7] This discovery also explained why the aircraft had such a vicious stall. Worse still, with the weight of fuel in the tip tanks, there was a distinct possibility of entering a spin from which the aircraft would probably not recover. A few days after this discovery, I had calmed down sufficiently to look at it objectively and it soon became obvious that the only solution was to completely rebuild the wing. On a positive note (the only one) and through careful inspection, I made sure that the rest of the airframe didn't have any other nasty surprises hidden away. I couldn't understand how that twist happened in the first place, but as the wing had to be rebuilt, I wasn't too concerned about that.

Halfway through stripping the wing, and *right*, a very bare wing

The wing was removed once again (not an easy operation at the best of times) and Roger Targett, of sailplane fame, agreed to keep it in his workshops and oversee the work. The wing itself was stripped in record time with the help of Steve Noujaim, his wife Anna and father-in-law Roy. It was both surprising and fascinating to see the wing structure untwisting itself as the outer metal skins came off. It soon became obvious that the reason for the twist was caused by a small jigging hole having been drilled in the wrong place. Reading through the build book it does say that *"when it comes to drilling these jigging holes, the builder needs to exercise the utmost care…"* somebody clearly hadn't. At last the puzzling fault was explained and the main load-bearing parts, the spars, could be used again, but unfortunately not the rest, not even the aileron. After ordering the parts from the factory, the long laborious build took place and by March 2005 it was back on the aircraft.

As the fuel tank itself had to be scrapped due to carrying some of the twist of the wing, I tried not to think too much of the time wasted cleaning flaking sealant and got down to building a new one.

Finally, attention was turned to the comfort of the pilot. Provision was made for a relief tube to the outside and a much appreciated item throughout the journey, the pilot's seat that Jill managed to make so comfortable.

And that, at last, was a completed aircraft ready to fly!

Chapter 2
FLYING AT LAST

Coming to the end of such a long engineering preparation had a curious feel. It was a mixture of the real and unreal, not unlike having a dream but not being asleep, being thirsty without wishing for a drink, arriving without having departed – a psychedelic clash of emotions!

There was a short wait for the necessary documents in the form of the 'permit to test' and then it was time to go flying. As the engine had just been built, it was necessary to 'run it in' and this clashed with the natural inclination to start cautiously with short easy steps. A new Lycoming piston-engine aircraft needs to be used at high power settings for the first fifty hours of use and especially so for the first three hours, when it needs to be run at very high power without stopping. This is in marked contrast to automotive practice and needs all other systems to behave without significant fault over those critical first three hours. The reward is an engine working at its optimum with minimal oil consumption.

The very first flight took place on 27th June 2005. Just in case things didn't go as well as intended, I wanted to ensure that there was a runway underneath me for the first half hour. Air traffic control (ATC) at Gloucestershire airport kindly agreed to my request to stay on the overhead of the airport until I was comfortable with the operation of all critical systems. The excitement of finally lining up on 04 runway had to be kept in check by the need for a clear analysing head to carry out the flight and check systems that had never flown before.

The need to adjust to a different performance envelope had an urgency that became obvious straight away. The first thirty minutes circling above Gloucestershire went a long way to allow me to catch up with myself. The performance was as good as had been hoped for and only a tendency to roll to the left required correcting, and this was rectified upon landing with relatively little effort. Verifying that the fruits of almost three years of labour lived up to my expectations was fantastically exciting and there was a serious danger that the huge grin across my face was going to stick permanently!

This first flight was the start of a new and exciting phase. Above everything else, I needed now to be an efficient test pilot and log as much data as possible. There was also more engineering work – checks had to be carried out between flights and the results of these flights were sometimes translated into experiments to explore new possibilities for further improvements.

Shortly after the first flight G-GDRV, or SLAVKA as the aircraft started to become known, had its first public showing. This was at the PFA Rally in Kemble airfield at the beginning of July 2005. The organisation, through their editor Brian Hope, generously provided me with a first class location. From this prime position, G-GDRV was the subject of a huge amount of interest and many admiring remarks, although some doubts were voiced about the sanity of the project! On balance, however, it was a very supportive occasion.

Airborne testing, late evening

One of the main objectives of the test-flying programme was to progressively increase the all-up weight to its new maximum while monitoring the performance and handling. The maximum weight of 907kg was reached in August 2005 and it was a success, despite the predicted blunted performance. To allow enough fuel usage to lower the overall weight from MTOW to MLW, the flight consisted of a circular route. I started from Gloucester, overhead Hull, via the east coast into Scotland, around Edinburgh and Glasgow, via the west coast to Liverpool and back to Gloucester. Four-and-three-quarter hours flying in order to land just inside the maximum allowable landing weight. It was a promising performance for the long stretches of water of the forthcoming circumnavigation. The flight at full weight was repeated a few days later as an independent check by the very talented and experienced Steve Noujaim. His findings confirmed my own observations and his report along with all my own test results were sent to the PFA applying for the full 'permit to fly'. 4th September 2005 saw the aircraft with all its paperwork ready to fly without restrictions, another great milestone left behind.

Having the aircraft with all the necessary documentation was effectively the step needed to finally expand the geographical limits of the preparation programme and actually 'go foreign'. The 'permit to test' only allowed flight over the British Isles and by having this restriction removed I was now able to cross reasonable long stretches of water and cover distances previously only possible by circular routes. Going around in small circles just doesn't have the same psychological impact as covering the same distance in a straight line. I had two main objectives for this part of the programme: the first was to build enough hours into the aircraft to come out of the initial running in period where teething problems are likely to arise; the second, a human one, to get into a long-distance frame of mind, to familiarise myself with the aircraft systems and learn to trust them.

The aircraft behaved itself admirably well, experiencing only a couple of problems with the autopilot. One happened on a trip to Switzerland and the resulting high friction on the elevator control did cause some anxiety on the way back. The other was an intermittent software problem with the altitude hold. Both these problems were quickly and efficiently sorted out by the manufacturers in the USA, whose attitude was refreshingly positive and gave me renewed confidence in their product.

At the eleventh hour a few aerodynamic improvements were introduced and they raised the fast cruise speed by a substantial margin. Although I am not so sure of how important they were at the planned lower speeds necessary to achieve maximum range, they were improvements none the less, even if not radical ones.

On the piloting side of things, the discovery of new landscapes, different regulations, different traffic controllers and all manner of challenges was incredibly exciting – after all, that's what started the whole thing. There were, of course, many details that needed sorting out, such as the need to be able to easily reach a great variety of things from the pilot seat. This led to an interesting scattering of pockets and Velcro patches for items varying from food and drink, through maps and sticky tape, to photo camera and batteries. Although some of these bits and pieces in isolation don't seem too important, on long solo flights they need to be just right, otherwise they risk becoming a major irritation. The only way to find out about these things is to actually do it.

Away from the cockpit, life was changing a great deal. In mid-2005 the conflict between the flight preparation and the pressures of business came to a critical point. The realisation that business was needing all my time and the preparation was equally requiring my undivided attention was leading to a lot of frustration and finally the inevitable conclusion came to me: I could only attempt to do one of these things properly. So, not for the first time, I went against common sense and took the momentous decision to close my business. This meant that on top of all the vast on-going preparation expenses and the rapidly approaching and potentially enormous flight expenses, I would no longer be generating an income. Jill was now going to bring the only wage to the household and that, together with our modest reserves, was going to have to do. 'The will to succeed is the most essential attribute to success' was about to be fully tested!

On the sponsorship front I was now able to add contributions from Executive Aviation Services with a most generous offer to use their hangar and from Gloucestershire airport with financial help and use of their prime facilities. There were also contributions from Consolidated Stainless Recycling, RGV Aviation, Rivers Fitness Rooms, Rehman & Sons and B Walker (Dursley). It was most encouraging to receive all this support.

However, there were still a few unwanted surprises in store. One of these was to discover, very late in the preparation process, that a passport visa was required for the USA. When previously I had looked at visa requirements within commonly-available check lists for tourism, I thought that British passport holders had no need for a visa to visit the United States. But I was wrong. This only applied if a traveller was to be transported by a recognised carrier, such as an airline or a shipping company. If the journey was to be undertaken by private aeroplane or yacht a visa is definitely required.

The process of acquiring that visa was not a particularly pleasant one, culminating with a trip to the US embassy in London, where I was expected to spend most of the day in a huge room full of other applicants and go through all manner of security checks. I had the definite feeling that the waiting room was regarded by embassy staff as full of potential terrorists, starting with myself. Meeting a delightful Iranian girl in the US embassy, with both charm and high academic qualifications, went a long way to lessen the ordeal and to prove that isolating ourselves from other cultures and people in the world is the best way to create misunderstandings – there's no us and them, we are all us! It is regrettable that the USA administration has such a huge problem with their perception of security and they exhibit a dubious way of going about it. However, despite the ordeal I was issued the required visa, sent to me by post a few days later.

Looking at the essential insurance aspects of the circumnavigating flight, there were great difficulties to overcome and again these came from unexpected sources – mainly insuring the flight over the USA. This issue was eventually solved most generously by my brokers, Traffords Ltd and Wellington Underwriters PLC. I simply cannot praise and recommend them enough and this is borne from experience and quite separate from their generous sponsorship.

At the very centre of the project was plotting the actual route that gave the project its physical form. The thinking behind this route centred on my strategy of trying to improve the record by spending less time on the ground than the current record holder, Hans Schmid. Because the performance of our two aircraft was quite similar my plan had to be based on making fewer stops. As his route had been considerably longer than the required minimum, I needed to consider a route not much longer than minimum to qualify for the official record. I had to cover at least 36,787.559 kilometres or 19,863.692 nautical miles to be precise. This was aimed at reducing my fatigue levels and, in turn, minimising the rest periods on the ground and therefore the total time spent travelling. Total time lapsed is the critical measure to calculating speed, there is no distinction between time on the ground and flying time. This also meant that the individual legs had to be as long as possible to avoid the inevitable delays when stopping. The simple fact that Hans Schmid was a Swissair captain and a confirmed successful long-distance solo flyer in the very aeroplane in which he had established the record, made the quest all the more awesome.

Other problems, such as where to find fuel or how to second guess the political situation around the globe were fantastic challenges in their own right. One difficulty that was not immediately apparent was the realisation that each flying day was going to be shorter by one-and-a-half hours compared to one day in a fixed location. This was because I would be travelling in an easterly direction, effectively going forward in local time. As the journey was going to happen in late winter or early spring, the already short days were going to be even shorter, not making life any easier. The search for a watch which was able to indicate both UTC time (GMT, for all practical purposes) and local time simultaneously was a high priority but I found a sensibly-priced watch advertised in a French aviation magazine – a modest investment that was to prove invaluable.

The actual route, as seen from the start, crossed Europe and the Mediterranean Sea into the Middle East with its huge deserts, and to the Indian Ocean. Here it would go around India and cross Thailand, Cambodia and Vietnam into the South China Sea and the Philippines. The route then entered the mighty Pacific Ocean, island-hopping to the USA and after overflying the American continent it finally crossed the Atlantic Ocean back home.

Closely related to this route, the paperwork necessary for the speed records I was going to attempt proved to be a task of phenomenal proportions. The format of these claims originated in a time when there was no alternative to paper forms, and each individual record needed three forms of its own to be filled in by the various control towers along the way. To further my difficulties, the initial setting up of my claims came at a particularly unfortunate time. The individual that for a very long time was in charge of the records administration of the Royal Aero Club retired in the middle of setting up my claims. Inevitably, his successor did not have the same relevant experience and it all became much harder than necessary – and expensive. These claims are not cheap and I feel quite certain that they are one reason why so few new records come from the UK.

Another aspect that creates big headaches for long-distance flyers is gaining clearances from the various aeronautical authorities to cross their airspace This has to be done for all the countries to be overflown in the planned flight. As each country has its own administration, they often have different procedures and just finding out whom to approach can be awfully difficult, as those that have done this before me can testify. After I decided on a finalised route, I approached a company that specialises in these matters, probably one of the best investments I made. The company was Overflight Ltd and they made it all look very easy.

As a lot of flight clearances have a limited validity period, it was essential to decide on a start date. From the middle of autumn 2005 onwards, a starting date for February 2006 was continuously talked about, so the end of that month it was going to be. There was a lot of urgency to comply with this self-inflicted deadline: too much delay had occurred over the years and I wouldn't accept another postponement. As it happened, there was going to be a very good case for delaying my departure and I was going to have plenty of opportunity to suffer the consequences of not having done so. At the beginning of February I picked up a particular nasty cold that developed into an infection of the upper respiratory tracks that still hadn't cleared completely by the end of the month. To push on with the departure dated 28th February in these circumstances was particularly stupid – any cold is a serious condition for a pilot and for a pilot who was about to push himself to the limit over this length of time it was not a clever decision!

The author at his departure party with wife Jill, daughter Natalie, and granddaughter Eva
(Photograph by Richard Crosby)

THE GREAT DAY ARRIVES!

Party time! All good things should start with a party.

On Friday 24th February 2006, I was joined by family, friends and sponsors in a celebration to mark the beginning of my great adventure. This party was held, appropriately enough, in the departure lounge of Gloucestershire airport and was combined with the press launch. It was comforting to see that there were so many people interested and concerned about both the project and myself. Being a solo effort, the actual experience of support and all the right 'vibes' were tremendously important – I suppose the memory of such support needs to last longer when you doing it alone.

This party reminded me of another occasion a couple of weeks beforehand, when some of my more experienced and accomplished pilot friends dedicated a lot of their time and effort to enlighten me with their wisdom and advice. Despite being most grateful, I feared that my decision not to implement all of their advice might have appeared as a snub. This was unfortunate as it was not like that, but there comes a point where you just have to go with your judgements. I took the opportunity to heed Polly Vacher's advice mentioned earlier. I hope the others have since understood.

The press launch was quite successful, despite some of the media not having done their homework. Somebody from a major media corporation thought it would be a good idea to install a camera in the cockpit to cover the entire event in a diary fashion. Great idea, but there was no way the hefty camera they had for me was going to fit inside my cockpit, in fact I think it would have been too cumbersome in the cockpit of an airliner! It was a missed opportunity and an obvious lack of planning on their part. Oh well, one less thing to worry about…

Like most elements of the project so far, this party carried a sting in the tail. It came in the form of a throwaway question from a pilot friend with huge aircraft ferrying experience, asking me if I had a 'TSC' for the USA as, apparently, nobody goes flying there without one. I had never even heard of it before, so the following day I was on the phone to Overflight frantically asking them to sort it out really fast. In the end I had to start without it and hope it would all sort itself out before I got to the United States. The actual document, a 'temporary security clearance', is deemed to be essential for any private aircraft entering the USA and requires exact dates and routes within the US – it is viewed by the Department of Homeland Security as critical to their policies. The pressure was decidedly increasing.

At last all that remained was to pack the survival kit and my own luggage in the aircraft. But, before that, I was going to have to find accommodation for my new little companion, my grand-daughter Eva's soft toy elephant aptly named by her mother as Philly (shortened and feminised from Phileas Fogg)! The survival kit consisted of a life jacket and life raft. The life jacket, always to be worn over water, had an emergency personal locator with a built-in GPS attached to it. In case of an emergency this would use satellite technology to relay a signal indicating my position and identification anywhere in the world. The one-man, ex-RAF survival raft came complete with drinking water, sickness pills, pyrotechnic distress flares, first aid kit and shark repellent (!) and was secured to the top of the large fuel tank right next to me so it would be instantly accessible.

This left my own personal luggage, which consisted of one single and very small (3kg weight) backpack with just one complete change of clothes, a toothbrush, a small tube of toothpaste and three disposable razors. Along with this, I was going to have to carry a laptop with all the navigational software, mobile and satellite phones and the software cartridges for the main GPS, as well as the required documents and the many forms for my record attempts. For outer clothes I would be wearing an ex-RAF flying suit as in my opinion it is the best there is for the purpose. The downside of this flying suit was the olive green colour. I really didn't want to look like a military person, but the thought of dying it pink, as somebody suggested, wasn't too appealing either. As I wasn't carrying a clothes peg for my nose, the plan was to wash all the 'undies' at every night stop and the flying suit at the longer stops.

So that was that. All I had to do was to wait for Tuesday and go. Wrong again! The satellite phone I had hired a few days before was found to have a faulty battery and this unfortunately prevented any testing of it in the actual aircraft. After a number of calls the replacement battery arrived Monday evening, just in time to charge it and hope it was going to work – this was going to be the only item that hadn't been thoroughly checked beforehand, but surely it wouldn't have another fault, would it? Time would tell…

Finally 28th February 2006 was here – the big day had arrived.

The route for the first day had been planned to head directly south from Gloucester, overhead Toulouse and Perpignan in the south of France and then south-east over the Mediterranean Sea to finish at Luqa in Malta. This course was chosen due to the uncertainties of the weather when overflying the Alps at that time of the year and limiting the actual flying distance. As conditions would have it, in the event some of the route still had to be re-planned at the last minute towards the French west coast to avoid the worst of a frontal weather system.

Getting up and ready in the early hours of the morning is not my kind of thing, but today it wasn't a problem. Not that I thought I was feeling nervous or overwhelmed by the occasion, but having not noticed the cold of the early morning and being strangely detached from events might have signified something else. The presence of Jill's oldest son, Matthew, was particularly comforting. He had re-arranged his work and commitments to support his mum at such an emotional time and this was especially generous as he had just started a new job and lives a long way from us, thank you Matthew.

We arrived at the airport at around 6.00 a.m. and the tangible feel of support exceeded all expectations. First of all my daughter Natalie was unexpectedly there despite having my four-month-old granddaughter at home. Then there were scores of friends filling the club house that had been opened just for the occasion. The airport normally only opens at 9.00 a.m., so the volunteered manning of the control tower to look after the departure and the airport reception to look after all the people and the media in particular was another delightful aspect of this experience. It was all quite stupendous. All those people braving the freezing weather to help out and wish me well so early on a February morning.

I had asked to be left in quiet concentration so, once the aircraft was checked out and pulled out of the hangar, it was time to say goodbyes to all in the club house. This was a momentous occasion. Interestingly, a long time after the event, there was a confession from someone present to the effect that it was thought that it may well have been the last time they saw me! Although nobody actually said so, there was a highly charged atmosphere. The only thing I could think of to break the nervous impasse was to announce that, "I'd better go and do it". Not the most eloquent of speeches, but concise and to the point – and all I could bring myself to say.

Walking back alone with Jill out of the hangar in the twilight of the early morning, the required single-mindedness for the task ahead had to share space in my head with the pressing concern both for Jill and Natalie. How they were going to cope and deal with the immediate events created a lot of anxiety, both by the fact I was the cause of the situation and, quite obviously, not being able to be around to help them. As we said our goodbyes and I strapped myself in the cockpit, the image of Jill walking away towards the gate to be able to see the actual take-off was curiously reassuring. Her silhouette walking away in her typical gait in a deliberate and steady manner, the glorious dawn gently breaking over the open spaces of the airfield and the overwhelming silence contributed to a perception of great beauty and calming influence in an odd sort of way. Then I was left in total silence and solitude. As I closed the canopy, the misting up of the glass due to the cold weather and the pre-dawn glow of light created an eerie atmosphere which all contributed to highlight the moment.

About to start, with Jill walking away *(Photograph by Richard Crosby)*

All these poetic thoughts were relegated to the back of my mind as the engine started with its glorious noise shattering the peace of the early morning. Chasing the Morning Sun was on!

The pilot in me then took over, the check list was slowly and carefully complied with, the radio checks carried out with the reassuring professional voice of Darren Lewington from the control tower and taxiing out to the hold of runway 27 showed all systems functioning correctly.

The take-off was carried out in the same professional manner, but the next couple of minutes weren't, sorry about that Darren! Turning 'downwind' into the most fantastic sunrise I could wish for, the need to go and wave at the crowd gathered just off the runway threshold did make me forget about asking clearance to carry out a rather unorthodox and low circuit. The following climb out into that sunrise and onto the top of a thin layer of stratus cloud was the absolute depiction of the Chasing the Morning Sun logo. What more could I ask for?

Chapter 3
THE FIRST LEG: GLOUCESTER TO MALTA

Reaching for that blue sky with the sun just rising above the horizon was the most beautiful sight any pilot could wish for at the start of a journey. But this wasn't just any journey, this was the start of Chasing the Morning Sun.

In the euphoria of this fantastic experience I simply couldn't resist a little mischief and I announced a 24,000 mile final approach to the runway I had just left. Darren's playful reply that, "at the moment you are number one in the traffic to land, report at three miles", was clearly better!

A cold view of the Dordogne

Upon entering the first controlled airspace at Brize Norton, their ATC was most enthusiastic, wishing the adventure the best of luck and I presumed Darren must have told them what G-GDRV was up to. Such encouragement was great for the morale and with beautiful weather of puffy broken cumulus clouds below and blue skies above, it was all running like a dream over southern England. It must be said that thoughts of how Jill and Natalie were faring did go some way to balance this wave of enthusiasm. An attempt to call Jill on the satellite phone was remarkably unsuccessful, leaving me to hope that the phone would perform better when talking to people who were used to poor radio communications. Above all else, I did have a mission to accomplish and the need to focus on that had to take priority over all other considerations.

Just as forecast, the beautiful weather didn't last long. Halfway across the English Channel between Goodwood and Deauville, clouds started forming over-head and quickly became overcast and their base lowered considerably. My arrival in France was decidedly gloomy with a cloud base of less than 2,000ft and the ground looking terribly soggy with most hills covered in a sprinkling of snow. The further south I flew, the lower the outside air temperature became, which was not the sort of thing that I had come to expect from flying in France.

It is fairly clear that the formation of ice on aircraft wings is a dangerous occurrence. Although often believed to be the consequence of the weight of the ice over a large surface, the most significant aspect of this hazard is the change of the wing profile and the drastic effect that such a change has on the lift required to maintain controllable flight.

Nearing the Loire valley, I found a layer of low cloud taking shape below me which went on gradually to merge with the upper layer, which eventually led to the formation of an unhealthy amount of ice on the wings with the outside temperature hovering around −4° C, ideal for this. The only sensible thing to do was to turn around through 180°, which I did and headed north again until a hole in the cloud allowed a spiral descent. The original heading was then resumed under a cloud base of some 1,200ft altitude with reasonable visibility between snow showers. The view of the French countryside was undoubtedly desolate with a strong westerly wind and winter abundantly in evidence. Passing Poitiers, the conditions started to improve and I was able to climb to a more sensible altitude, although the outside temperature kept on falling. As usual, French ATC was excellent; Paris Information giving a flight information service (FIS) supplemented by radar information, was always a comforting backup.

At Toulouse my track turned left alongside the beautiful snow-covered Pyrenean mountain range. The outside air temperature was now −10°C. The view all around was quite magnificent with majestic mountains and a fantastic combination of snowy peaks, dense, dark forests and glistening water running in deep valleys. Crossing one last ridge, the mountainous splendour was suddenly replaced by the approaching sight of the Mediterranean Sea with the city of Perpignan near its coast and the outside air temperature jumping to a positive figure for the first time since crossing the English Channel.

After leaving the French south coast I was handed over to Spanish ATC and once clear of some military danger areas I turned south-east on a direct track to Malta. This was the first substantial sea crossing of the adventure with 680nm of sea to overfly to Malta and only some 60nm of Sardinian land to cross along the way. The stiff breeze coming from the Pyrenees remained with me for a long time with three obvious consequences. First of all the sea surface was very choppy and the possibility of having to ditch into those conditions wasn't appealing. Secondly and on a much more positive note, the ground speed rose to a whisker off a very impressive 200 knots, despite maintaining a very conservative air speed of 150 knots. This, if it was to remain like that, was going to compensate for the delays of the icing episode. Thirdly, the 'wave' effect created by that wind over the Pyrenees was felt as a rising and lowering motion for an extremely long distance, no doubt helped by the smooth sea surface. At least waves from the atmosphere are preferable to the ones of the Mediterranean!

Once communications with the Spanish ATC came to an end, the next frequency for an Italian ATC didn't give any results for a long time. This is because VHF radio can only propagate in straight lines and does not follow the curvature of the earth. It was the first time I was out of radio range and although I wasn't unduly worried, I was aware that this situation wasn't exactly ideal if I had to ask for help in an emergency. Dialling the international emergency frequency into the radio standby window seemed a good idea, as this frequency is always monitored by ships and airliners.

Normal communications resumed on approaching Sardinia and the anticipated views of the mountains barely revealed themselves to me as the island was wrapped in cloud, and I was only able to catch occasional glimpses of its rugged landscape. One of those glimpses showed Capo Carbonara, which with a name so closely related to food, triggered a realisation I had not yet eaten anything. My mind had been wandering. Clearly time to dip into my high-energy food supply and sort myself out.

Left: One of the few sightings of Sardinia
Above: Sicily

Leaving Sardinia under the control of Rome FIS, I was required to execute a slight wiggle to avoid a military danger area and it was then straight on to Malta. Passing a few miles to the south of Sicily, I was surprised to see the extraordinarily flat western part of an island that is so notorious for its mountains and some of its notable inhabitants. Those mountains were completely hidden by cloud and, from what I saw, Sicily could have been as flat as Holland. It must be said I felt somewhat miffed by missing these impressive landmarks.

The island of Gozo finally came into view, with its larger twin island of Malta behind and looking equally beautiful, literally dazzling with the late afternoon sunlight reflecting off its 300ft high white cliffs. Malta ATC, most welcoming and surprisingly aware of my flight objectives, was kind enough to go as far as asking which way I would prefer to fly towards the airport. Without really knowing which way would have been more interesting, I elected to go around the southern coast to see the island to my left as it is convention that the captain or sole pilot occupies the left seat of a fixed-wing aircraft, therefore giving a better view in that direction. This decision was rewarded with a stupendous picture of the island and then, on the final approach to Luqa airport, I had a first-class view of the historical and beautiful port of Valetta.

As Malta is two hours ahead of England, it was already 5.00 p.m. local time when I landed, meaning that I had to contend with a terrible forward visibility caused by the very low-setting sun shining straight in my eyes as I lined up with a westerly runway. The actual landing was at 15.02 UTC giving an average speed of 149.3kts (276.6kmh) for the GC distance of 1,195nm (2,213km). The actual distance flown was considerably greater at just over 1,300nm (2,407km).

So there I was, the first leg completed, in the middle of a pleasantly warm Mediterranean island after the cold and ice of northern Europe, having achieved a convincing world speed record for the first leg of the journey. I couldn't have wished for a better way to start this adventure.

Malta

Upon landing, I was directed to the far side of the airport, where the handling agent was waiting to marshal me into a parking slot on a very large, empty and windy apron. This was my first contact with handling agents at international airports and watching the arrival of my support crew with three cars, two vans and a fuel bowser for my little aeroplane was staggering. I knew only too well who was going to have to foot the bill for all that activity! The actual agent representative, Godfrey, was very efficient and went all out to accommodate my requirements, including gaining the required access to the tower in order to have my record forms stamped. This was not the easiest thing to do as, since '9/11', control towers in international airports are viewed as high security areas and Godfrey's help was therefore particularly appreciated. The controllers in the tower, as I had already experienced over the radio, were very enthusiastic about the flight and wanted to know all the details of this adventure which was very flattering, but also took up a lot of precious time.

Godfrey arranged accommodation and transport to a pleasant, comfortable and curiously 'old world' hotel. Arriving there and going to the rather formal restaurant in my flying suit complete with four bar epaulettes raised a few eyebrows. This was the sort of place where decorum and service niceties had precedent over everything else and the ambience was enhanced by lights that could be at best described as 'romantic' and at worst, very dim. The balance of the whole place was not only disturbed by my attire but much more harshly by the mobile phone going off in my pocket. As all eyes glared at me, I managed to swiftly switch it off and pretend it was nothing to do with me, but little did I know a greater predicament was still to come in the form of an innocent menu. The menu itself wasn't a problem, but having left my clear glasses in the aircraft was – reading such things without glasses in poor light was by now only a distant memory. All I had on me were my very dark sunglasses, which were fine when landing into a very low sun and not too much of a problem in daylight, but very dark glasses coupled with the dim light made reading a menu pretty well impossible. This was a lesson I wasn't going to forget in a rush. I didn't actually have to resort to pointing at dishes on the menu and hoping for the best, but not far off.

Only when I got back to my room did I dare to switch on my mobile phone again to find that the call that had caused such a stir in the restaurant had come from Jill, hoping to further our earlier brief chat reporting my arrival at the airport. After swapping tales about all the excitement of the day, she went on to tell me that a picture of the aircraft taxiing in Malta had been published on the internet, possibly even before I had parked. The wonders of technology!

The likelihood of a good sleep before the 4.00 a.m. local start was completely lost within half an hour of turning off the light when the phone rang again. This time it was a friend in Birmingham asking me when I was going to start my world flight! Words to the effect of "go away, I am in Malta and trying to sleep", had the desired effect, but kept me awake afterwards. So much for the chance of a good rest…

Chapter 4
MALTA TO LUXOR

When the alarm went off at the end of that restless night, it was merely signalling that I could stop trying to sleep. I didn't have any sleep worth mentioning, but it was time to get up just the same. After an invigorating shower I enjoyed a specially-prepared full breakfast at 4.30 a.m. At times like this, good old fashioned service really is appreciated and welcome.

After being collected punctually from the hotel as arranged, it was time to experience the downside of the handling agent services, time to pay. The landing fee from the airport came to a very reasonable £6, the handling fee to a not so reasonable US$314/£170, very different from all my previous experiences, but not a complete surprise.

The flight plan I had filed to Egypt started the route eastbound towards the western tip of Crete, then turning south to the Egyptian coast, over the pyramids and down the Nile valley to Luxor. The straight route would have been, of course, to overfly a corner of Libya, but although Gadaffi & Co were at that time seen as quite good guys, Libya still had a lot of restrictions to flights and I felt it was simply easier to take the longer sea route.

Taking off from Luqa's 32 runway soon after sunrise I turned east along the south coast towards the first turn-point of Paleochora VOR in Crete.[8] This gave me a new view of the countryside, taking me over pretty white-washed houses dotted around the island, brightly lit by the early morning sunlight. However soon after leaving Malta behind I came across a nearly-full cloud cover, soon to be unbroken, between 1,500ft and 4,000ft of altitude. After climbing through a little rain I reached beautiful sunshine on top of the clouds. Here I enjoyed a very healthy tailwind component giving a ground speed of 190kts before climbing further to 9,000ft in order to keep clear of some military exercise going on in that part of the Mediterranean.

As the distance to the first turn-point in Crete was 450nm (833km), I knew that VFR communications were soon going to be lost, so this was a good time to see if the satellite phone was going to be of any use for the really long sea crossings. It jolly well wasn't. Ringing Luqa tower back in Malta gave me quite good reception, but only to hear them saying they couldn't hear me! They eventually worked out who I was, but clearly couldn't understand anything I said. This was most likely due to the poor quality of the microphone provided in the kit that just wasn't capable of coping with the background noise, no matter how well I tried to shield it. The only possible use for the satellite phone was that it might work on land, possibly on remote islands where conventional cell-phones would not be supported by a network. The HF radio was definitely going to be needed, although at that time I had yet to permanently install the long aerial that is essential for its use.

I eventually got in touch with Messinia ATC in Greece via the VHF radio, who went on to liaise with the Egyptian authorities regarding the progression of my flight plan. It soon became apparent that things weren't going to be easy. First I was informed that Egyptian ATC had requested Messinia to send me past the eastern end of Crete and then to turn south towards their coast. As this was going to increase my total distance by a substantial amount, I had to indicate my disagreement and, possibly exaggerating a little, told them that such an increase in distance was going to compromise my fuel margin. After what seemed a long wait, Messinia came back to me saying that the Egyptians were allowing the flight to proceed as per the flight plan but at FL125 (12,500ft), which again I had to decline as this clearance altitude was higher than my own absolute ceiling of 10,000ft. This limit was due to my decision not to carry oxygen and G-RV does not have a pressurised cabin. Eventually they agreed to allow the flight to proceed at FL085 (8,500ft). All this took place over an inordinate amount of time and in the meanwhile, I had overflown the turn-point in Crete and was well on my way towards the Egyptian coast before the clearance was resolved. Crete was a magnificent sight with its high mountains of over 7,000ft covered with a thick coating of snow. All I could see of the island was that brilliant mountainous whiteness above an equally bright cloud blanket, creating a beautiful and unexpected spectacle. I certainly never expected to see so much snow in the middle of the Mediterranean Sea!

Approaching Egypt the cloud cover completely dissipated and as the sea gradually became shallower towards the coast, it allowed a myriad of marine colours to go from a beautiful shade of blue through turquoise to green, giving an astonishingly kaleidoscopic display to the passing pilot. And I was that lucky pilot. The contrast between that colourful spectacle and the sudden change to uniform desert brown was shockingly abrupt, to say the least. Another marked change was being transferred from the co-operative Greek controllers to their less than compromising Egyptian counterparts. Soon after crossing the coast, I was directed away from my intended route, but only aware of the new route as far as the next VOR beacon, therefore leaving me with no idea of their overall intentions. This process repeated itself a couple of times and as a result I didn't go anywhere near my sightseeing spots. Instead I was forced to fly a route parallel and to the west of the Nile, through a mild dust storm up to about 8,000ft. When I could see the ground at all, I found it fantastically rugged but quite unfriendly – a pilot needing an emergency landing certainly would have found it hostile. I was particularly glad not to have found myself in need of such a landing, as given a choice, I think I would have preferred to ditch into the sea than trying my luck onto those sharp and tightly-laid rocks.

While enjoying this 'mystery tour' (and in a funny sort of way I was enjoying it, as this was very much part of the great discovering experience of this adventure) the outside air temperature rose towards 17°C at 8,000ft, making the cockpit extremely hot. This was aggravated by the sun shining through the 'greenhouse' canopy making it feel pretty sticky, despite the portable window shades I was using to minimise that effect. The previous night's lack of sleep combined with the heat made keeping my eyes open quite difficult. Fortunately there was an unexpected and fully automated way to wake me up: every time I dozed off I stopped hearing the engine! That was a certain way to wake up really quickly and to stay awake for a good time afterwards. To date I don't have a totally satisfactory explanation for this, all I know is that every time my eyelids shut under the weight of sleep, I stopped hearing the engine noise – amazing.

Eventually Cairo ATC put me on to a direct eastbound track to Luxor into a worsening visibility, particularly as I had to start my descent into the thick of the sand storm. While this was going on it was curious to note that most nations use their own language for radio communications between themselves. It is not only the French that appear to refuse to use the international aeronautical version of English as widely be-moaned in England.

My only sighting of the Nile was a very quick glimpse of that giant of a river just as I was absolutely vertically overhead, on 'left base' for Luxor airport. As I was looking for a single runway in the 020° direction, I was more than a little puzzled when confronted by not one, but two runways, equal and parallel. It didn't take too long to work out that I was looking at one runway and one equally large taxiway, but which one was which was a different matter. Aiming the aircraft at the centre of the airfield did eventually allow me to pick up enough clues as to which was the real runway and to an uneventful landing onto African soil. The actual figures were 07.40 hours elapsed time to bridge the GC distance of 1,118nm (2,071km) and about an extra 100nm (185km) actual distance covered. Very satisfactory and another possible record.

Taxiing towards a huge and under-occupied apron in a very dusty airport, I was greeted by my Egyptian agent representative, Sayed and an even greater number of vehicles than in Malta. This time I even had one of those very large airport buses to carry me and my little bag – time to fear for the wallet being severely hit. The refueller arrived with a lorry which was on its last legs and presented a fuel nozzle that was clearly designed for the old propliners of the fifties and their phenomenally large tanks. So much so that this nozzle was actually larger than some of my fuel tank filler apertures! This wasn't helped by the actual operator, a chap of advancing years, advanced waistline and generally looking like a heart attack waiting to happen. As this apparently impending cardiac catastrophe monopolised all his attention, there wasn't much spare capacity to take care of the job in hand, so even the cockpit ended up with a gallon or so of Avgas.

While the handling people were working out fuel invoices and the like, I rigged up the HF aerial to see how it was going to stand the next leg over the Saudi desert. I had the distinct impression that this work of mine was viewed by my entourage with a degree of suspicion and puzzlement.

Getting through the formalities such as customs took a great deal of time but not a lot of effort as Sayed and his side-kick dealt with all that was needed to be done. Despite the fact that the huge airport building was completely devoid of people, it was nevertheless a pleasant place to sit and wait as it was air-conditioned and the marbled waiting areas were furnished with reasonably-comfortable seats. The only bureaucracy that required my personal intervention was the flight planning, the Met report for the following day and the dreaded record forms to be signed by ATC in the control tower.

The flight planning was not so good. My proposed VFR route to Muscat wasn't acceptable as all flights in that part of the world have to exclusively utilise airways, forcing me to redraw my complete route. The Met Office was rather unusual to my western eyes, it seemed that the person looking after it lived there all the time, as he was asleep in a bed next to a table with the remains of a recent meal. If he didn't live there, he worked inordinately long shifts! The control tower was accessed without too much trouble and the controllers were very friendly, wanting to know all about the adventure and insisting that I had tea with them. All very pleasant but again time consuming.

Eventually Sayed arranged an aircrew rate with the Hilton hotel and a taxi to ferry me there and back. This was most welcome as I was going to be able to enjoy the use of a comfortable room (which I had deemed necessary to enable me to maintain such a tight schedule) and the bonus of a modest price. I felt sure that the drive there was at least partially alongside the Nile, although it was impossible to tell for certain as by then the blanket of a pitch-black night had fallen over Luxor. It was a fascinating African night teeming with life in an Africa-meets-Asia sort of way. I suppose that the essence of Egypt is just that, a transition from Africa into Asia, with a bustle and habits originating from the East, but firmly rooted in the African continent. The hotel proved to be as comfortable as expected and the aircrew rate most welcome. Could this have been the only real advantage of my four bar captain epaulettes?

Dinner was in the hotel's excellent self-service restaurant overlooking the Nile, or at least I might have been overlooking the Nile if the outside had been lit up. After dinner the really important task, other than telephoning Jill, was to go through the new route and build up all the necessary data and charts into my Jeppesen FliteStar software and print out the results for use in the cockpit. This excellent software is very good and I found it invaluable during the whole adventure. However it does have one significant shortcoming as when trying to print the results, it doesn't allow the opening of its files in a computer that isn't running the same software. There is the unofficial and tortuous way of saving the results into a PDF file, but this obviously relies on finding a computer with Acrobat Reader installed. The Hilton's computer in Luxor didn't, so I was stuck until somebody in reception suggested that I could go to the internet café across the main road.

Walking out of the hotel's private drive and through the manned security gate put me squarely into another world with the bustle of a real Egyptian town and without any tourist presence. The donkey carts, the light car traffic, a few lorries and splendid lively activity seemed miles away from the Hilton a few yards back down the drive. Although I probably ought to have been a little more apprehensive about my very conspicuous appearance in a flying suit, I felt quite safe and not at all the 'local oddity', despite it being around 11.00 p.m. The internet café was run by a young 'can-do' type of guy who was as helpful as anybody could wish for. Despite his helpfulness, his computers didn't have Acrobat Reader and the version I did manage to download with a very slow connection (despite his opinion to the contrary) was too old to support my files and the whole exercise was not a success.

Back in my room, pen and paper came to the rescue and I made the notes I thought were necessary for the following day's navigation. The down-side to all this was that by the time these notes were written and the underwear was washed, it was after midnight and I had to be back at the airport by 4.30 a.m.. To add insult to injury, I managed to lose all the pictures I had taken that day while downloading them into the laptop. I was not happy about that.

Time to try to squeeze two nights' worth of sleep into three hours...

Chapter 5
LUXOR TO MUSCAT

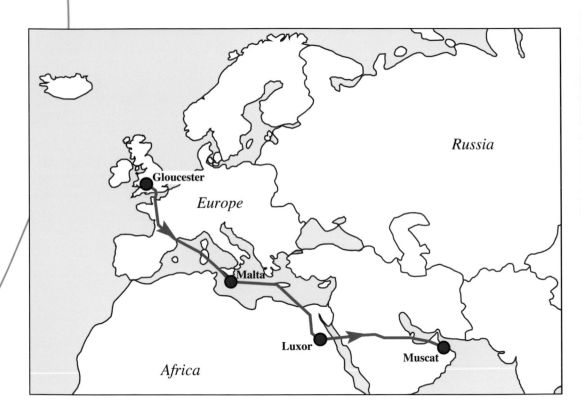

With only three hours available to sleep, I was paranoid about not waking up on time. To make sure there was no chance of oversleeping, I set the alarm on the cell phone, placed an alarm call with reception and set the alarm clock in the room, all at five minutes intervals from each other. This was not as simple as it sounds as the cell phone was set for GMT and everything else for local time. The increased margin for error wasn't conducive to relaxation. My preoccupation, added to the adrenaline already flowing from the excitement of this adventure, meant I woke up startled a number of times throughout the night, invariably thinking I was flying and hearing the engine stop.

It might have been a broken short sleep, but unlike the day before, at least it was a sleep.

Although the hotel didn't serve breakfast that early, I was able to buy a boxed picnic from reception and the essential large bottle of mineral water.

The taxi arranged by Sayed arrived punctually to take me back to the airport, but as it was still the middle of the night, yet again not even a glimpse of the Nile. Once through the deserted customs and immigration areas, it was time for the agent's invoice, which at US$401/£217 felt rather steep. However it covered landing fees, parking fees, taxi fares and the hotel room. Not a bargain, but not so bad after all.

Going down from the upper level of the airport building to the ground floor, I found myself in a small lift along with two other people. One of them told me that, "Mr M… would like some dollars". The situation didn't look too good – we were in a ghostly-empty building, Mr M. was a very overweight official in customs uniform and the other occupant of the lift closed the doors again once we arrived at the lower floor. I interpreted this, possibly unfairly, as a threat, although it must be said that nothing untoward was said or happened. A few Egyptian pounds, of no further use to me, were gratefully received by Mr M. and the situation evaporated.

After carrying out the pre-flight inspection with Sayed for company, he asked if I wasn't forgetting to remove the wire (the HF aerial) I had installed on one side of the aircraft the previous evening – I think this had been seen as some sort of security device! Had they thought it was a trip wire? Anyway, soon after first light I was taxiing out to the runway with a visibility as poor as on the previous day and now aggravated by a rising sun shining straight into my eyes.

The original clearance was given initially to airway intersection 'IMRAD' and as I didn't know where that point was exactly, it showed up a problem I was going to experience for the rest of that day, as I didn't have any IFR charts for that part of the world. This was because I hadn't been able to print the files from my lap top the previous night. All I could do was make an educated guess that IMRAD was where my track crossed the border with Saudi Arabia and act accordingly. As it happened the guess was good, the border was halfway across the Red Sea.

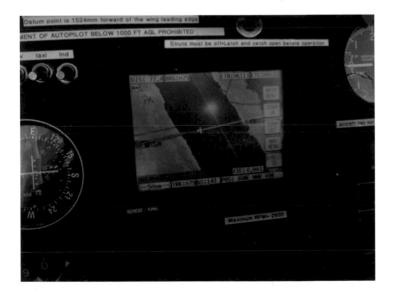

Approaching the Egypt-Saudi border

The first radio service I used in Saudi Arabia was Madinah, very efficient and accommodating, which was contrary to what I had heard in the UK about Saudi ATC. If anything, visibility was getting worse and there were long periods of IMC, where all I could see was brown dust surrounding me up to about 10,000ft, which was my altitude limit.

As there wasn't much to see outside, it was a good opportunity to have my breakfast from the Hilton picnic. This was in an ideally-sized box for an RV-6 in-flight meal and the contents were very nice too. It did strike me that being able to relax enough to have breakfast in IMC must have proved that my instrument training had worked.

Every now and then I was able to view the desert below and it was absolutely fascinating – much more interesting than I ever thought a desert could possibly be. First of all there were many tall, rugged and tightly-packed mountains clearly making some of those areas virtually inaccessible from the ground and any thoughts of an emergency landing almost laughable. Amongst these mountains, the sight of a large extinct volcano of a perfect cone shape was totally unexpected and a highlight of the journey.

On a few occasions I could see small groups of horsemen with their shapes in stark contrast to the uniformity of the desert. Concentrating a little more on their movements revealed dust tracks barely discernible from their surrounds. And allowing my gaze to follow those tracks I discovered some settlements, usually sheltered by large hills. These amazingly well-camouflaged tiny villages, clearly built of local materials and without a single motor vehicle to be seen, were exactly the same shade of light brown as everything else and invisible from the air without the benefit of other clues. These hidden outposts have to be a magnificent testament to the resilience and character of their inhabitants, living in such a hostile environment hundreds of miles away from any of the supporting infrastructures which we consider essential. My mind went into overdrive trying to visualise the life, the social structures and the beliefs of these wonderfully-isolated people. This was the first occasion in this adventure that I knew my life would have been enriched if I had been able to stop and share a little of their life and environment, so completely different from my own. But no time for that, there were records to chase and flights to fly, to say nothing of nowhere to land.

A few hours later these thoughts were once again stirred by the sight of enormous irrigation fields situated in some of the flat parts of the desert and nowhere near any obvious source of water. These great circles of luscious green were a veritable monument to the ingenuity, persistence and indomitable spirit of those that created and maintained them, facing the most difficult natural conditions to cultivate crops. Realising that we enjoy an ideal environment for that very purpose in the UK, but turn our backs on it by buying crops from thousand of miles away suddenly appeared to be complete madness! Have we lost the ability to take advantage of our gifts from nature, or is our 'developed' way of life marching to oblivion?

A substantial number of FIS in Saudi Arabia are military and these were particularly diffi-

Opposite: An extinct Saudi volcano
Left: Irrigation field in the Saudi desert, through air thick with dust
Below: An island full of oil equipment

cult to deal with as their operators nearly always had a poor understanding of English and their accents were extremely hard to decipher. Worse still, nearly every time I was passed from one FIS to another my route was changed. This led to me spending a great deal of time re-calculating and re-plotting, only to have the route changed again as soon as I reported to the next FIS, and so on, for what appeared an infinity. On top of this my sunglasses, obviously designed to deal with the bright light, were much too dark to be reading into the comparatively shaded lower cockpit, and gave me a huge headache. On a more positive note, while all this work was taking place, there was remarkably little turbulence at the level I was flying, FL095 (approx. 9,500ft). This was more than could be said about some airliners requesting to change flight levels to escape turbulence, an unusual role reversal.

These changes to the route resulted in my exiting Saudi Arabia further north than planned, actually overhead Dhahran and towards the island of Bahrain in the United Arab Emirates (UAE). Air traffic controllers in the UAE sounded as if English was their first language, which greatly helped the quality of communications. These controllers were also quite accommodating in giving me a direct route to Muscat once I told them that my fuel margins had been eroded by the multiple re-routings.

The view was then dominated by the Persian Gulf. It is difficult to overfly this notorious body of water without thinking of all the conflicts of interest and fighting in this part of the world. The motivation for these conflicts was very much in evidence as I overflew a small island completely covered in the paraphernalia of the oil industry.

Coasting in from the Gulf at Abu Dhabi, the terrain had some fantastic mountain formations sculptured by eroding winds, giving an appearance of giant walls snaking through the arid countryside. So much for my previously held idea of the desert just being gently undulating sand dunes.

The last 200nm (370km) towards Muscat were made more pleasant by the lowering of the blazing sun and slightly cooler temperatures. However the lack of sleep, the extremely hot conditions up to that point and the concentration and effort to keep up with all the changes throughout the day had contributed to a high level of fatigue. The prospect of the next day's twelve hours flying to get to Sri Lanka before the following evening wasn't too appealing without the opportunity for some sleep. To establish a clear dividing line between 'go and no-go' that night, I decided that if I could arrive in Muscat before sunset, I would do my best to have a short sleep in the airport and carry on, otherwise I would leave it for the following day.

After a final straight approach to Muscat of some 90nm (166km) parallel to the beautiful coast of the Gulf of Oman and the contrasting stark beauty of the mountain range on the other side, 08 runway of Muscat International Airport awaited me. As I turned off the runway into the taxiway, I couldn't help myself marvelling at the warm red glow of the mountains and the surrounding airport. This was caused by the magnificent huge red setting sun, or to be more precise, an exact semicircle of sun showing above the horizon – this exactly coincided with my dividing line whether or not to go immediately to Sri Lanka. No passing of the buck to natural events then. I just had to make my own decision and from previous experience with bureaucracy and form-filling for speed records, I knew that I wouldn't have had time to sleep at all before leaving. Today's flight had already covered a GC distance of 1,398nm (2,589km) over nine hours and twenty-three minutes at an excellent average of 150kt (278kmh), the longest flight so far. This had created a fatigue level that, along with my lingering cold, meant I was in no fit state to fly an aeroplane for another twelve hours. The decision to rest that night had to be taken.

The task of my handling agent for that evening was considerably easier than his predecessors in previous days as I was postponing the signing of forms in the control tower and the fuel wasn't going to be uplifted until the night of departure. The fuel tanks needed to be filled only after the heat of the day subsided, otherwise the inevitable expansion would lead to a great deal of fuel being lost overboard. Clearing customs and immigration appeared to be made smoother by the gold bars and flying suit and it was then only a matter of finding a taxi to the Intercontinental Hotel. According to a friend of mine, it was the hotel to stay in in Muscat.

Muscat was a revelation. I was expecting a rich city, but what I saw was above all expectation. All the taxis were new and immaculate, taxi drivers were impeccably attired in Arab robes and roads were new and beautifully laid out. I saw no litter, no decay and the buildings along the highways towards the hotel were unspoiled and often amazingly sumptuous in an extrovert fashion simply not seen in Europe. The main mosque and the national bank were extraordinary buildings, literally covered in gold and illuminated in a most effective and spectacular manner. The hotel at the end of the taxi ride was very much in keeping with all this, in fact it could be described as an extravagantly-built modern palace. It soon became obvious that my friend either benefited from paid expenses or is even richer than I thought. The most basic room was over US$300/£162 per night.

Once settled into my room and connected to the internet, I opened the phenomenal number of supportive emails that were such a fantastic boost to my morale. There was also the only malicious email I received in the entire journey and another one from Overflight telling me that my clearance through Vietnam was now subject to a minimum altitude of 26,000ft. This was completely outside my flight envelope and therefore a lot of re-planning and clearance negotiations were going to have to take place. Just as well I had decided to stop over in Muscat. A few attempts at using the satellite phone to ring Jill only served to confirm the set as useless, the more conventional telephones therefore got a good bashing in the billing department.

Taking a look at the two restaurants in the hotel, I tried the Mexican-themed one, as the alternative was a buffet type and I am not an enthusiast of 'self-service', even if it has a five-star rating. I found it a curious experience, the service was good with efficient Philippine staff, the food was well-prepared, the furniture of good quality and the live music was reasonable, but it did not amount to a great restaurant.

The full benefit of my expensive bed wasn't fully realised as, in what was rapidly becoming a familiar pattern, my sleep was interrupted by waking up startled at regular intervals. The tension of the whole adventure and adrenaline were doing their best to prevent relaxation. At least I enjoyed the luxury of being able to wait for the light of day to raise from the king-size bed as, instead of flying, the main task for the day was to sort out the route around the Vietnamese problem. The navigation software was enormously helpful to find an alternative and I was able to send a flight plan to Overflight before breakfast, so they could consider the necessary clearances and advise me accordingly.

After breakfast I was able to indulge myself with a stroll on an almost deserted, long, curving beach with the Arabian Sea gently lapping at the light smooth sand. This beach constituted the shore of a wide bay in front of Muscat. With beautiful white buildings as a background, the warmth of the Omani climate, the sub-tropical vegetation and distant fishermen curiously pulling ashore their nets from the sea with four wheel drive pick-ups, this created a fabulous picture of being somewhere really remote, pleasant and foreign. Having got there with my own little

Opposite: A view from my room in Muscat
Above: The silent beauty of Muscat bay

aeroplane in three days, after stopping at two other exotic locations, each in their own continent, was simply mind blowing! That my luggage restrictions didn't allow for swimming trunks was a definite minus point.

But enough of holiday. Time to go and ring my friend Martin Courage who knows all about Penang in Malaysia as this had now become my intermediate destination on the way to Manila, in order to avoid Vietnam. Once suitably enlightened about Malaysia, I rang Overflight back only to learn that a clearance for Indonesia was now a major problem within the available time. A little re-arranging of the route avoided Indonesia altogether, despite a penalty of an extra 150nm (280km) and that should have been all that was required for this last-minute alternative.

I still had to attend to all the things that were left to do at the airport. After a taxi ride back there late in the afternoon, I had occasion to test my skills at getting through the security system without the benefit of the handling agent, whom I couldn't raise on the telephone. This was another occasion where the 'official' appearance probably helped. After a few barriers I found myself in an office at the base of the tower, sorting the signatures for the record claims and the flight plan for the departure for Colombo in Sri Lanka in the early hours of the following morning. All was going swimmingly well until the chief of security turned up in a fluster. It transpired that aircrew are not allowed airside without a permanent escort and as far as access to aeroplanes was concerned, a police presence is required and there is no contact allowed with anybody there, not even talking to the crew of an aeroplane parked in the next slot!

It took a while for the security chief to come to terms with me actually being there and accept that he couldn't turn the clock back. And quite some time before he came to the conclusion that the only way forward was to find the handling agent and whatever security required for me to go to the aircraft in order to check it and have it refuelled. While this was taking place, a B-N Islander air taxi from the Maldives crewed by two female pilots and using the same handling agent, came to park in a slot close to mine. Assuming (incorrectly, as it transpired later) they had just arrived from the Maldives, which are next door to my destination, I was more than keen to hear from them about the meteorological conditions on the way. However having dared to walk a dozen steps away from my aeroplane in their direction nearly gave the agent a heart attack and the jitters to all the security staff around there. Security was clearly a major issue and my questions unfortunately had to remain unasked.

Returning to the hotel again in the dark, Oman still dazzled me with its opulence, but there was a niggling doubt in the back of my mind about all that splendour being propped up by a stifling security; the total absence of beggars added some fuel to those thoughts. I do realise that such a short stay in cosseted conditions does not give enough material to draw any real conclusions, but I wondered for a while about the heavy-handed security.

Back at the hotel it was time for an early dinner in the buffet restaurant, as I had already sampled it at lunch time and found it preferable to the Mexican one – despite my self-service misgivings.

While wandering around plate in hand and choosing from the excellent and varied buffet on offer, a charming American lady came over and following a chat over the hors-d'oeuvres, invited me to join her and her brother at their table. She clearly had been sent to ask me over to their table simply because they assumed I was some sort of high ranking RAF officer. So much for the thought that my irresistible good looks were the attraction! Big brother was a major in the US Army and was in that part of the world working for his government, introducing himself as – "Major Smith, United States Army – Sir!" This was an unparalleled opportunity to have a challenging exchange of ideas, but the potential to offend people was too high and I did my best to restrict the conversation to tourist attractions. Despite my pleas to the contrary, Major Smith couldn't help himself punctuating phrases with "Sir!", very much reminding me of some of the reasons why I chose to be in civvy-street. An interesting time, cut short by the need to rest by all concerned – they had driven hundreds of miles in the heat of the desert and I was going to have to be up at 2.00 a.m. local, ready to fly the twelve hours to Colombo.

Chapter 6
MUSCAT TO COLOMBO

At 2.00 a.m. the second alarm rang without me having heard the first one. Jumping out of bed panicked, it took me a while before realising I had muddled up local and UTC times, and I wasn't late at all.

The packed picnic waiting for me in reception came in an enormous box and was only up-staged by the size of the bill for the room, a formidable US$750/£406 – wow.

The whole bureaucratic procedure through the airport was handled very efficiently by all concerned and the handling agent bill came to US$185/£100, including landing, parking and take-off (!) charges. The only problem was their lack of familiarity with the light end of General Aviation (GA). This is something that can appear surprising for inexperienced global pilots like myself, but not at all unusual when away from affluent Europe, and the even more affluent USA. There was also a bit of an issue with the departure clearance and eventually I had to accept the only possible option with a minimum height of 15,000ft.

The climb out before dawn was soon getting me in trouble due to the clearance requirement and my own oxygen-less restriction of 10,000ft. At one time, as I might have 'accidentally' switched off the transponder altitude reporting mode 'C', ATC was telling me that they would have to direct me to return to Muscat if this couldn't be resumed. Upon reporting that my full fuel weight wouldn't allow for an early landing and eventually correcting the transponder issue, they appeared to resign themselves to let me get on with it and leave their airspace as soon as possible. Upon reaching Oman's boundary, I was instructed to contact Mumbai on HF and was left to enjoy a splendid sunrise over the Indian Ocean.

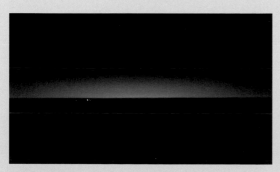

Spectacular sunrise over the Indian Ocean

The HF communications with Mumbai were almost impossible, mainly because my HF microphone wasn't correctly set. Apart from these technical difficulties, this was also the first time I had to deal with real time HF communications since my theoretical studies and exam. The volume of traffic and the quality of transmissions in these frequencies were even worse than I had anticipated. By the time I sorted out the microphone, I could no longer reach Mumbai on the allocated frequencies. I was then faced with the longest sea crossing to date (1697nm/3,143km actual distance) without being in touch with a ground station, a fact that was dulled by a terrible sleepiness in the middle of the day. This was not good and thoughts of a snooze for ten minutes or so had to be dismissed. I just couldn't bring myself to trust the alarm to wake me up after such a short time when I felt in desperate need of at least ten hours sleep. Fortunately I had some caffeine strips for this very reason and was able to enjoy the view of the exceptionally calm surface of the Indian Ocean and ponder the huge distance I was crossing. In the depths of my mind I used to regard the Indian Ocean as 'a bit of water at the bottom of Asia', when in fact, the distance I was travelling from Muscat to Colombo is nearly the same as that from Canada to Ireland, and that does not even take into consideration the eastern part of the ocean!

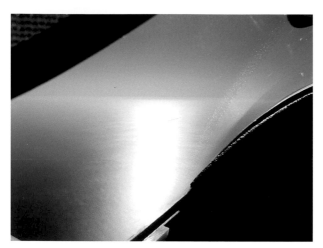

The huge picnic box from Muscat, taking up most of the floor area of my luggage bay, supplied enough interesting food to alleviate the monotony and having the luxury of 'real food' was a treat. While fighting sleep and general tiredness, I learnt that regular food and drink is a very effective way to combat fatigue. However, this was no help for the lingering effects of my cold, which was becoming rather worrying and I was beginning to feel that my thinking capacity was being blunted by it.

Once the sun had risen above the horizon enough to enable me to look ahead without being permanently dazzled, the completely cloudless sky allowed an amazing view of the ocean's surface. It appeared to have an unusual texture, not unlike a gigantic coarse blue linen table cloth extending to the horizon in all directions. It was a completely uniform blue, not at all broken or varied. From my height there wasn't even any hint of waves, which was consistent with the wind at the surface being very light, as made obvious by the smoke of the odd tanker I overflew. I still have no idea why the ocean had this 'textured water' appearance, but that image made a great impression on me. Mind you, the concept of a beautiful 'watery grave' did also cross my mind more than once!

While this stunning sight was passing under my wings, the business of flying carried on, greatly helped by the technology surrounding me. The autopilot kept faithfully following the route loaded into the GPS and it was working without any glitches. The HF aerial, as noticed in the previous flying day, was creating a little extra drag on the port side and that required a tiny amount of right rudder to be constantly held to obtain maximum performance. For those interested in these matters, the slip ball was just touching the line of its 'cage', hardly crossing it at all, but centring it gave a measurable increase in speed. To achieve this balance over such long flights I found myself having to alternatively use the right foot, the left foot and even both feet together to lightly load the right rudder pedal. Not an ideal situation, but it worked.

Soon after midday local time, the splendidly cloud-free air started to give way to scattered cumulus clouds below me at some 4,000ft, suggesting there was a much greater build-up in the making. This was both expected and unwanted. Sri Lanka is very close to the equator, in fact the latitude of Colombo is just 7° 10′ north. This situation on the globe's surface and the effect from the local mountains mean that thunder clouds form during the afternoon and the inevitable spectacular thunderstorm happens at around 5.00 p.m. local. As my start from Muscat had been somewhat delayed, this was going to coincide with the time I was planning to arrive in Colombo. And of course the monumental thunderstorm clouds (CBs, cumulus nimbus) were there extending left and right as far as the eye could see some fifty miles from Colombo airport and completely barring my track to the safety of its runway.

The presence of CBs everywhere was particularly bad. A CB has a huge amount of energy and an aeroplane, any aeroplane, entering one of these clouds has got an excellent chance of being spat out in bits. My named alternative diversion airport was also the other side of that threatening wall of black and other possible alternatives were going to be a long way away, far enough to put me well into the night and not being able to see those CBs. Not a great choice, so I decided that the best course of action was to go down below the base of these CBs at much reduced speed and, if there was a choice, aim for what looked the least frightening part. Some humorous relief was provided by Colombo ATC when they asked if the aircraft was weather radar-equipped – they had obviously never seen an RV-6!

Opposite: Hundreds and hundreds of Indian Ocean miles
Above: The start of the cloud gathering
Below: The darkness of the moments before the storm

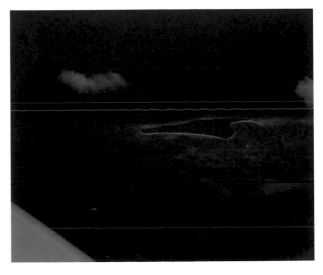

The base of these CB clouds appeared to be at around 1,500ft, although with the torrential rain coming out of them it was quite difficult to be too sure of what was where. It had to be a matter of looking for an area slightly less dark than the rest and going for it. The sound of all that water hitting the airframe was just unbelievable, the resulting 'whoosh' completely masked the noise of the engine, something I had never experienced before – in fact something I didn't believe was possible.

It has to be remembered that the engine of an RV has a capacity of 320cu in (about 5,250cc) and the unsilenced exhausts finish just below my right foot, so it needs an awful lot of noise to completely cover it. Fortunately everything kept running as designed and not much water entered the cockpit. Normally water tightness is not one of G-RV's best qualities and it proved that the many hours spent rectifying this were indeed well spent. After some ten long minutes I came out of the waterfall in the sky and the very helpful Colombo ATC vectored me into a soaking, but beautifully welcoming runway.

Opening the canopy next to the handling agent's mini-bus sent all the water resting on it into the avionics area and thankfully demonstrating that the second line of waterproofing was also up to the job. The flight had taken eleven hours and fifty-two minutes to bridge the distance of 1,587nm (2,939km) GC at an average of 134kt (248kmh), another potential record. I was glad to hear that the agents were expecting my arrival and assured me that they had collected the necessary fuel barrels from the domestic airport, as the international airport only stocked Jet fuel. Before we could attend to the refuelling, there was the bureaucracy to sort out and I was unlucky to be further delayed by having arrived just before a staff shift change. The only positive outcome of these delays was that by the time the refuelling could start, the rain had stopped and the additional discomfort of getting soaked was avoided. This refuelling was a new experience as it was carried out from the back of a small pick-up truck with a hand pump and, as expected, I had to purchase whole drums. This meant I had to leave behind some seventy litres of fully paid for fuel, as there was no space for it in my tanks. I am sure somebody ran some road vehicle at my expense for a while! Oddly enough, despite the actual cost, I didn't really mind, Sri Lankans are so helpful, hospitable and kind that I prefer to see such a situation as an opportunity to return their kindness, even if it was not entirely voluntary on my part. The fuel itself was quite reasonably priced at US$1.50/£0.81 a litre.

The records claim forms were even more of a problem than on previous occasions, not necessarily because of the usual tedious international issues, but due to their own serious domestic civil problems. This happens mainly in the north of the country, but places like this airport were heavily guarded with check points within the actual airport manned by armed soldiers. The extremely helpful handling agent representative did his best to ease our way past these check points, but it all took an amazingly long time. The sharp end of a Kalashnikov is an excellent tool to promote patience! Once up in the tower, all the controllers were most enthusiastic and interested in what I was trying to achieve, so it was a shame that I didn't have more time to enjoy their company.

The Taj Hotel, as arranged by the handling agents, was about fifteen minutes of terrifying driving from the airport. Driving in Sri Lanka has always been a hair-raising experience, but at least it used to be conducted slowly enough to give a reasonable chance of survival in the inevitable-looking but miraculously-avoided accidents – but now they had discovered speed.

The hotel wasn't as good as I had hoped, the service was full of promises that weren't followed up and the supposedly twenty-four-hour restaurant was closing, just about managing to produce some indifferent fish and chips after a long wait. While waiting for the fish to cook and wondering if they were in fact having difficulty in catching it, Jill and I had a long talk on the telephone about the record claim forms. The insistence of the Royal Aero Club to get them signed by the control tower of the airports I was visiting was simply no longer realistic in 2006. The days of just wandering into control towers of international airports are long gone and it is only becoming more difficult with the passing of time. Personally, my big problem with this situation was having to suffer it every day. I think I was spending longer dealing with this issue than I was spending resting from some ten hours flying. This was simply not a sustainable situation and I was starting to think that the records simply didn't justify getting myself into a state of complete exhaustion. Jill's offer to talk to the RAeC to see if the situation could be improved was most welcome.

I finally got to bed just after half past midnight to be at the airport at four in the morning.

Chapter 7
COLOMBO TO PENANG

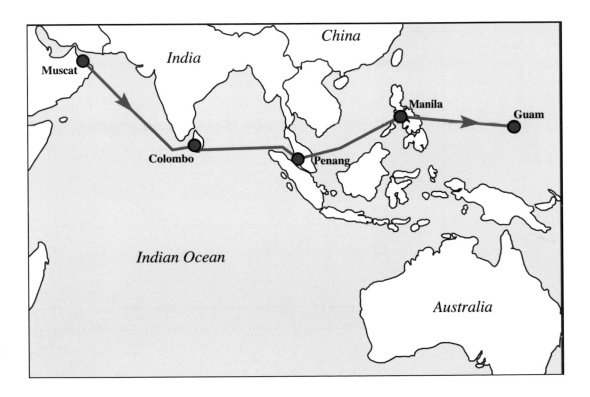

The day didn't start well. Nobody in the hotel reception seemed capable or willing to produce the arranged transport to the airport. In contrast to previous days, I was not the only one waiting for the shuttle. Watching my fellow travellers resigning themselves to waiting in silence, I had to resort to some forceful talking and was eventually rewarded by the arrival of the mini-bus.

Once in the airport terminal, things didn't improve. The telephone number I had for the handling agents was unavailable and with their desk unattended as anticipated, I simply had to wait for someone to turn up. On the positive side I had time to recover from the death-defying drive from the hotel and could indulge in people-watching, always a favourite pastime of mine in far away places, made especially interesting by the astonishing number of people in the terminal at such an early hour (4.30 a.m. local). The humidity, however, was not pleasant, so much so that the lenses of my glasses kept misting up in the non air-conditioned terminal. Later on I found that at five in the morning the ambient temperature was 22°C and the dew point was 21°C.

Once the handling agent representative arrived everything started to happen as it should and dealing with the bureaucracy to leave the country was remarkably painless. I paid the handling fee of US$60/£33 for a most willing service along with a landing fee of US$12/£6.50, both the cheapest so far and by far.

Once that was attended to, I was able to go to the aircraft without any further delays, where I found the inside of the canopy completely covered in condensation, a further indication of the very nearly saturated atmosphere signifying a very high risk of carb ice. Carb ice, or carburettor ice, can form when the humidity is high and at temperatures up to the mid 20°s Celsius. This ice can in fact cause the engine to stop.

Preoccupied with these thoughts, I nearly forgot to replace the cartridge in the main GPS holding the aeronautical mapping data for the rest of the journey as far as the Americas. Almost forgotten, but not quite!

I took off from Colombo into the pre-dawn light with a few cumulus clouds just clearing the tops of the mountains. Another thin broken layer of strato-cumulus higher up was illuminated by a fabulous orange light of the morning sun not yet risen. The spectacle of light and dark gave a mysterious atmosphere to that beautiful island – only the thought of carb ice kept a reality check on me.

The coast of Sri Lanka after take-off

Just prior to coasting out to the south-east, I caught a glimpse of the town of Galle to the south-west, reminding me of the terrible events caused by the tsunami only fourteen months previously. Galle was where I first fell in love with Sri Lanka. So what had happened to all those I met over there, to their families, to the children that had become adults, to their houses, their jobs and businesses? From that height and distance it all seemed peaceful and beautiful, but what about at ground level? How were people recovering from such a tragedy, and finding the motivation to simply carry on? So many questions and the coast just sliding by underneath was not giving any answers.

The memory of the spectacular thunderstorms of the previous day made me feel a little uneasy about the forthcoming arrival at Penang, a destination that not only was closer to the equator, but was also surrounded by hills. Although these thoughts were in conflict with the weather forecast, I couldn't just completely ignore them.

Soon after coasting out Colombo ATC was anxious to establish a two-way HF communications while still in VHF range, making me feel they were taking my well-being as their personal responsibility. Having somebody actually concerned about the progression of the flight, as opposed to simply carrying out a job, was comforting and my regular calls to report 'normal operation' were actually something to look forward to.

It was during this part of the journey that I first experienced a significant and constant head wind. At around 15kt, the headwind was not enough to make me unduly concerned because the GC distance was 'only' 1,221nm (2,261km). Nevertheless it was still enough to slow the ground speed to levels I hadn't yet experienced in this adventure. This lower ground speed however gave me more time to observe nature and think.

Passing some distance to the north of Banda Aceh after six-and-a-half hours of flying from Sri Lanka, the magnitude of the tsunami hit me. The Banda Aceh peninsula was, of course, at the epicentre of the earthquake that created the devastating tsunami of Boxing Day 2004. Realising I had been travelling at a very swift 140kts air speed for six hours and thirty minutes in my relatively fast and modern aircraft, it was most humbling to acknowledge that the tsunami took less than a third of that time to cover the same distance in the opposite direction, with

> The effect of wind on ground speed is often seen as an alien concept. Riding a bicycle into or out of a stiff wind makes a huge difference to the effort required. However if said bicycle is travelling at 10mph it will remain travelling at this speed providing there is enough power available. This is the result of travelling over a stationary ground, but an aircraft travels through the air and this is rarely stationary. Using the bicycle analogy, it is not unlike riding along a moving walkway – if, as before you are riding at 10mph in the same direction of the 3mph moving walkway your ground speed is 13mph. Conversely, if you are riding against the direction of the walkway, your ground speed will be 7mph. Flying into or out of wind is much the same. The calculations get much more interesting when there is a relative angle to the wind other than 0° or 180°.

an energy vastly superior to several nuclear explosions. For all of man's self-perceived achievements, Mother Nature can and does continually demonstrate just how insignificant we are in the great scheme of things. Just to reinforce the point, all of Sumatra was at that moment hidden under monumental CB clouds and I only knew it was there because it ought to be and the GPS said so – I never saw any of it. Being alone in a small aircraft over these huge distances provided the ideal circumstances in which to appreciate the power of natural forces.

There was a definite feeling of isolation once the transition of HF radio coverage took place from Colombo, with its parental care, to Chennai, formerly Madras. The latter displayed no particular concern about the progress of the flight, but showed an unhealthy interest in my personal details. Although I can't actually recall being asked about the inside leg measurement, I certainly remember their obsession with commercial considerations, such as to whom they could possibly send an invoice. Such exchanges made an easy victim of correct radio procedures and I couldn't help thinking that if there had been somebody out there in distress, they would simply have had to wait for their turn to speak!

The presence of all those thunderstorms over Sumatra did not physically affect me because I had my planned route to avoid their airspace altogether and remain over international waters. I came close to a number of other easily-avoided isolated CBs that gave the journey a break from the continuous blue above and blue below.

The last 300nm were flown between Sumatra and the Malaysian peninsula with the final 90nm around a fairly complex system of danger areas under the control of Butterworth Approach, the military base situated just 15nm away from Penang International. The visibility towards the destination deteriorated markedly for the last half hour and the vectoring from Butterworth was most welcome. At least it was up to the point of the overhead of Penang when it became apparent that they didn't seem to appreciate that this was a VFR flight, and I didn't have the IFR plates for Penang. I couldn't say I was too happy with being on the overhead of the airfield with 9,000ft in the altimeter. It turned out that the procedure over there is to descend under the control of Butterworth and change to Penang tower's frequency once established on final to the runway in use. Several requests to descend were flatly denied and I eventually found myself on a 2.5nm final stretch at 5,000ft above the height of the airfield. It was a good job that the runway was 11,000ft (3,350 metres) long as I found myself crossing the threshold at 120kts (65kts is the norm) but still with plenty of time to slow down, deploy flaps and land well within the length of the runway.

The time for this leg was ten hours and ten minutes for a GC distance of 1,221nm/(2,261km) giving a speed of 121kts (222kmh). This reflected the headwind and the dog-leg route to avoid Sumatra, adding 150nm (278km) to the journey, but I was happy with that.

Taxiing towards the terminal buildings, I was directed to the GA parking area, something that surprised me by its mere existence. There were a couple of Citation jets and, behind the hedge of what appeared to be a local flying club a Cessna 172 was parked. After tying down G-RV in the pleasantly hot evening, a couple of airport officials drove over and arranged pretty much everything for me. This included going to the terminal to change a little money to cover the very modest landing fee that I had to pay in the local currency, arranging for the fuel truck to come over, recommending a hotel nearby and explaining the unusual process of hiring a taxi in Penang. All attempts at tipping to show my gratitude were politely and firmly refused. Just the other side of the security fence, my arrival was proving to be the object of a fascinating spectacle for a young family– I suppose they found me and my RV very unusual!

The fuel bowser arrived promptly, displaying great efficiency and delivering the lowest priced Avgas so far – US$0.91/£0.49 per litre. The combined landing and parking fees came to £1.88 and the joint arrival and departure navigational fees to £3.55. Better still, they were quite happy to allow me to sort myself out without the assistance of any handling agents and their associated fees, a refreshing change after the somewhat high charges I had been paying up to this point. As the information I might need was freely available it was a nice change to be able to do my own thing. My own thing involved, as always, going to the control tower to get the dreaded signatures for the record claims. The snag here was that Penang airport has the tallest tower I had visited and the elevator had a notice saying it was out of service! The notice was right and the spiral stairs were steep and long. Once I arrived at the top and recovered my breath, I met the two controllers who were most pleasant, helpful, informative and interested in what I was doing. It was noteworthy that one of them was a female, the first I had met on this trip. After the much easier and speedier tackling of the stairs with gravity in my favour, it was time to go to the terminal to clear customs and immigration as by then I really wanted to find the recommended hotel and a restaurant. With only my cereal bars and water since getting up at 3.00 a.m. (local), I was starving.

Clearing customs was not quite as smooth as I might have wished. Until then I had always been provided by the local customs officers with the essential 'general declaration' form, however in Penang they didn't have any spare forms and appeared to be quite upset by my inability to produce one myself. After much searching of filing cabinets and desks, they resorted to photocopying an existing form with all the filled-in answers individually covered up with meticulously cut-out pieces of paper! Once this was sorted out I was given my aircrew immigration document and was free to go. As I had been informed, getting a taxi in Penang's airport is somewhat different from most places. First I had to queue at a 'taxi desk' in the terminal building where I bought a ticket and only then could I go to the taxi rank and use the ticket to hail and pay for the taxi. I thought the female driver was further evidence of enlightened freedom and equality of the sexes in this far eastern country. Possibly due to her circumference greatly exceeding her height, she had adjusted her seat right back and unbelievably low, so much so that I simply couldn't imagine how she could steer us out of trouble in an emergency, which I am glad to say didn't happen.

The hotel was about a twenty-minute drive from the airport and was comfortable and pleasant, but didn't have a restaurant open at that hour of the night. Fortunately the pretty and smiley receptionist was able to give me directions to an Indian restaurant within walking distance. Trying to ring Jill on the way there I was further frustrated by the satellite phone which, despite displaying a good signal, just couldn't keep working for more than a minute at a time before the horrible piece of junk lost its signal. Only the thought of the £1,000 penalty for not returning it to the hire company saved it from a nearby skip.

The Indian restaurant appeared to be the only thing open around there at that time of the night and it was very large and busy with tables inside and out. The food on offer came mainly from the permanent BBQ outside, but my choice was rather limited by the lack of a common language and my overriding need to not be too adventurous with what I ate. A 'Delhi belly' is something not to be contemplated in the confines of a small cockpit! Everybody was most helpful and although I was the only westerner, I never felt out of place. I did enjoy being in that restaurant, my hunger possibly made the food taste even better, and it was ridiculously cheap. I made my way back to the hotel and wrote in my diary about Penang: 'Not at all a feel of third world country about it, a place worth spending some time in.'

I got to bed a little after midnight for a 4.30 a.m. departure.

Chapter 8
PENANG TO MANILA

Checking out of the hotel before sunrise, I was once again unable to acquire a picnic box, which didn't surprise me as upon my arrival the whole hotel was closed for the night, with the sole exception of the reception itself. I had started to suspect that buying picnic boxes from hotels away from the Arab states was going to be difficult and in the fullness of time I was proved right. This was indeed a shame, the availability of 'real' food in the confines of a cockpit over long periods of time was a fantastic boost to the mind as well as the body.

The taxi I had booked to take me back to the airport turned up on time and in the early dawn light I liked what I saw of Penang Island. As I had only found myself there due to the last-minute problems with the Vietnamese clearance, I considered myself very fortunate to have had the opportunity to see this lovely country, even if my visit only lasted a grand total of twelve hours.

Upon arriving at the airport, I was aware that I was leaving this gentle country behind the automatic doors and I was entering the people-churning machine that all major airports have now become. In fact the outlook was distinctly gloomy because, as they had no scheduled commercial flights departing that early, customs and immigration were closed. After much discussion with the policemen looking after security, I was allowed to go through to airside on the understanding that I would be coming back to attend to the bureaucracies, as by the time I was likely to be ready to fly the airport would be fully staffed. It was certainly an unorthodox approach, nearly as unorthodox as the way to airside which had no security checks of any sorts. I simply went through the public areas and at the end of a building there was an unmarked and unlocked door that led to a deserted staircase and out onto airside – just like that! It was a refreshing change in a world of security paranoia.

While carrying out my pre-flight checks to the aircraft, it occurred to me that the forecast headwind for the whole leg to Manila, as checked on the internet from my hotel room, was going to reduce my fuel reserves to a lower level than usual. This was not ideal, but easily fixable, particularly in view of the low price of Avgas in Penang. A quick radio call to the tower had the bowser arriving once again without delay, however this time the price of the fuel had gone up by a massive 25%! The language barrier prevented me from finding out how the increase came about and, more to the point negated any sort of negotiation. However, it was still cheaper than in most places…

I was glad there was no need to go to the top of the tower again, that could well have used most of my energy to fly the onward 1,350nm (2,500km) to Manila. It was quite tempting to 'forget' to go back to clear customs and immigration, but in the event it all went smoothly, even if clearing those formalities coming from airside and going back to airside felt a little strange.

Walking back through the public areas, I found the airport starting to look alive and there were places open to serve food, which led to the high point of the morning: the luxury of being able to eat breakfast. Marvellous.

Taxiing out to the runway created a lot of interest from the crew of a FedEx 737 doing the same thing. As pilots they could appreciate this type of flight more than most and they weren't too shy in taking up radio time to say so and favourably comment on the aircraft – thanks for the morale boost, guys.

The initial climb out was fairly sedate in view of the high temperature, humidity and full tanks of Avgas. This gentle climb gave me more time to enjoy the view over the misty hills with the kind of tropical light that helped to give the heavily-wooded countryside a great eastern charm. Possibly the sort of eastern charm so many westerners – including this one – fall in love with. The privilege of being able to fly your own aircraft relatively low over such wonderful places really is breathtaking at times like this. There just isn't a better way of enjoying and living such an experience.

My initial track crossed the irregular shape of the Malaysian/Thai border a few times on the way to the north coast; despite following the obvious airway I had to track a course of my own to stay clear of Vietnamese airspace. VHF communications went without a hitch, but once I transferred to HF, they became quite difficult. At first I received a good service from Singapore, despite being muffled in patches, but in the latter part of the flight radio communications with Manila became exceptionally awkward. And it has to be said that some operators were distinctly more difficult than others.

Above: The Thai-Malasian border
Below: The mystery island in the wrong place

This part of the journey was a milestone of the whole adventure. The Indian Ocean had been left behind and I was flying over new seas, in fact in crossing the South China Sea, the name alone sounded more exotic to a European like myself. This sea was my first encounter with the mighty Pacific Ocean and as I had always perceived the Pacific as the single biggest physical obstacle of my entire route, I was definitely in awe of the occasion.

The weather remained clear, with a few cumulus clouds well below my now customary flight level of 9,500ft. The cockpit was very hot due to the greenhouse effect of the canopy glazing and the outside air temperature was 15° to 17°C, instead of the −5°C expected at that height in 'standard atmosphere' conditions. Every now and then I came close to a CB or TCU (towering cumulus), but not close enough to be a problem. Soon after crossing the border of the Manila FIR, the sight of a beautiful and isolated teardrop-shaped island to my left provided much needed visual stimula-

tion. In particular the usual light blue of the water changed through all shades of turquoise until it reached the pure white sand of the shore. It was however not as stimulating as the realisation that this island, according to the GPS, should have been out to starboard instead of port! I still have no idea whether this was a glitch in the GPS mapping or something else, such as the island shown on my screen being hidden from my view by clouds – but it is always a navigational 'issue' if features don't appear where they are expected…

I was suddenly aware of a tremendous amount of heat around my feet and, oddly enough, I remembered that it had also happened to a lesser extent the day before at about the same time in late afternoon. Vast amounts of heat being felt within a specific part of the cockpit suddenly and for no apparent reason, is more than enough cause for alarm. Eventually I arrived at the conclusion that it was simply due to my black socks. Late in the afternoon the sun shone from behind and straight onto my ankles and as the colour black absorbs heat, they were getting very hot indeed! Light coloured socks would have been better, but unfortunately I didn't have any with me.

Once I had established that there wasn't a fire, I indulged in a little experiment to calculate sunset time by the most basic method and tools. This was motivated by the fact that I was approaching Manila with some two hours to run, but with the sun already rather low in the horizon, I wasn't sure if I was going to arrive there before or after nightfall. So, as I had no pressing priority tasks at the time, instead of just looking up the relevant data in the GPS, I thought it would be more fun to calculate the time of sunset with the shadow of a pencil and simple trigonometry. As an aside, I felt quite certain that the reason so many navigational methods were developed in the early days of long-range sailing was not only because there was a critical dependency on the results for survival, but also as much to do with having plenty of available time to occupy the mind with that sort of exercise. However the results were inconclusive as sunset was due at about the same time as my expected arrival and it could have been day or, er…, night! However, at least it was correctly calculated, as obligingly supported by the actual sunset – it had just gone dark as I landed in Manila International Airport.

My final approach into Manila was through a lot of cloud surrounding the actual island and I was glad of the ILS during that phase of the flight. The cloud obviously contributed to a much darker evening and gave the bay to the west of Manila and just short of the runway, an air of great beauty. As I flew very low over numerous moored sailing boats, the water showed a myriad of reflections from all types of lights, as would be expected from such a huge city.

Clearing the runway I was directed to a deserted and poorly-lit apron where some customs officials were waiting for me. These were led by a lady officer, and they were all very elegant in immaculate white uniforms and apparently more concerned with talking about the flight and having their picture taken with me and the aircraft than anything else.

The flight had taken ten hours and twenty-seven minutes to cover 1,385nm (2,565km) at an average of 128.52kt (238kmh), having been slowed down by the headwind and the deviation to clear Vietnamese airspace.

After meeting with the customs officials, I was cleared to taxi to the hangar of the handling agent but this was no fun at all. This far into my journey, the seat cushion had settled a fair amount making looking ahead over the cowling and to the right over the life raft pretty much impossible. This situation was worsened by the poorly-illuminated taxiways in Manila airport. To make the matter harder, one link of the tailwheel steering (the actual mechanism that allows steering on the ground) had broken on landing and the very long and uncertain distance to the hangar necessitated heavy use of differential braking to overcome this problem. Not an easy time.

When I eventually arrived at the hangar, there were several people waiting for me and I got the impression they were expecting to carry out the scheduled fifty-hour maintenance, previously arranged by Overflight, there and then. I was alarmed to find out that they didn't have any service items and they weren't confident about the likelihood of getting any the following day. I also had the impression they had been waiting for me for many hours, despite the flight plan showing my arrival time.

Pushing the aircraft into the hangar, it became obvious that the brakes were incredibly hot, indicated both by the smell of overheated linings and the actual temperature of the wheel fairings; it was not a good sign. The hangar was populated with a few private light aircraft such as a Cessna 152, Beech Bonanza and an Augusta helicopter, the latter obviously having some major work carried out as it was devoid of rotors and a few other large parts.

While we were discussing what needed to be done and somebody took my passport to be stamped by the appropriate authorities, a USA-registered King Air twin-engined aircraft also arrived at the hangar from an internal flight. It turned out that this aircraft was subcontracted to the US Army, apparently, "getting their people in and out of remote places", all over the Philippines. A charming crew member talked enthusiastically about my flight and most evasively about theirs!

Having established my insistence on being present before work commenced in the morning, that I really wanted top grade oil and that washing the oil filter was definitely out of the question, the maintenance guys got me a taxi to a hotel of their recommendation. Their negotiations carried out in Filipino for the price of the taxi were capped by their words to the effect that if the driver didn't behave and charged more than 50 pesos, I was to let them know and they would 'sort him out'! I wasn't too sure how to take that, although it occurred to me that extra vigilance was a good idea.

Chapter 9
THE MANILA EPISODE

As I had no idea what to expect from the hotel I had been taken to, it was good to find that the five-star Heritage Hotel was large, modern, pleasant and well-staffed both in numbers and in quality. By the time I had checked in and dropped my bag into the comfortable room, the only eating place available was a self-service Chinese restaurant, which wouldn't have been my first choice – a prejudice born completely out of my ignorance of oriental cuisine. However, this turned out to be a pleasant experience: the food was prepared on demand, right in front of the customer and it was very good. The staff were most helpful and the restaurant itself was of a very high standard as its rating would suggest and at US$30/£16 all inclusive, was excellent value for money.

The possibility of a decent sleep in a comfortable air-conditioned room was something to look forward to, particularly as my cold hadn't really improved and my bronchial passages were busy clearing themselves of horrible gunge. Another piece of good news, brought about through Jill's efforts with the RAeC, was that they had agreed that my record forms no longer necessarily needed to be signed by the control towers at the airports I was visiting. They could now be signed by other, easier to access, entities such as handling agents. This would certainly make my life much easier and possibly even allow for some rest at night!

The following morning, rested and breakfasted, I was directed to the hotel's own taxi desk just outside the door and informed of the 600 pesos taxi fare for the reverse of the journey that had cost me just 50 pesos the night before. Outraged at this, I went to find my own taxi and agreed on a 200 pesos fare with the driver. This turned out to be a bad idea. Some independent taxi drivers appeared to be simply pimps using the taxi facility to reach their potential market and were not too good at understanding the subtle nuances of the word NO. Traffic in the rush hour made the previous night's ride look lightening fast and it was astonishing to see a huge human mass flowing around the city in all directions, along with the most varied motor vehicles imaginable. I didn't see any accidents, but I was constantly being distracted by my driver's constant offers of 'nice ladies'. When he eventually gave up on that, he went on to asking if there was anything else I wanted, tapping me on the knee, as if there was something else on offer… Fortunately, by then we had arrived at the airport and the conversation turned towards how he was going to get me change from a nearby petrol station after I got out! Eventually the security guard from the airport came over and managed to solve the change problem – the final settlement came to 300 pesos.

Arriving in the hangar, I was greeted by the chief engineer with the news that the port brake had completely failed, as demonstrated by a puddle of hydraulic fluid around the wheel, no doubt caused by the previous night's abuse. Fortunately, they had the necessary seal and tools to carry

out the repair and they had also come up with the correct oil filter and Shell W100 oil, not pre-
cisely what I had asked for, but perfectly adequate for the conditions ahead. It turned out that the
engineering team were dedicated, knowledgeable and flexible and they carried out the repairs to
an excellent standard, despite being devoid of the most basic spares. Not having a new washer to
replace a lost one was one such example. Where they found a used one I don't know and I didn't
ask, but find one they did and they completed all the necessary jobs to my total satisfaction.

While supervising and helping with the maintenance work, I met two of the most colourful
characters of the flying community in Manila. The first was Joy Roa, owner of Air ADS Aviation,
my handling agents and maintenance organisation. Joy was 'Mister Fix-it' in that part of the world
and knew everybody, had flown everything and ran the place with great flair and style, leaving
his people to do the menial work. I thought that Air ADS might have seen more affluent days
but that wasn't any reason to shy away from style! Joy spoke to all manner of people regarding
my clearances to Guam, as it was not obvious how to satisfy the USA authorities regarding the
many aspects of security and customs, on top of air traffic issues. Events were very slow to develop
and the vast time differences between Manila, Guam, USA and the UK didn't help.

The other great character was Luc Helgen, a French citizen, long-time resident in the Philippines and the owner of the YAK 40 parked outside the hangar. This had given me some trouble
the previous night, as I had been informed that the hangar I was looking for had a YAK aircraft
parked outside. To me, they were radial-engined, old Russian aeroplanes and for the life of me I
couldn't see anything like that anywhere. This YAK was a smallish jet airliner and I wasn't even
aware of their existence. Monsieur Helgen was an outpost of 'Frenchness' in this remote country
and offered the most interesting contrast to the 'Brit' equivalent. He appeared to be an entrepre-
neur of great charm, clearly enjoying life in the tropics and was having some of these YAK 40s
refurbished for his inter-island air service. His view of the Philippines was most favourable, regrettably something I had difficulty in recognising from my limited experience.

Going back to Joy's office, there was little development to further my progress with the US
bureaucracy and the thought of carrying on irrespective of the consequences didn't appeal to me.
The US military have a poor reputation with episodes of so-called 'friendly fire' and as Guam was
home to a particularly important military base, I didn't fancy the idea of becoming an impromptu
airborne target for the local F-16 fighters. On balance, I had to accept that I would have to wait
another day for the security clearances, even if this was eating into the time margins for the world
record. While we were having this discussion, Joy had a visitor in the office in the form of a retired
air force general. He was also one of the most fascinating characters that I met in Manila. As well
as having had one of the highest positions in the Filipino air force, he was also a colourful entre-
preneur with a host of 'hands on' projects such as kit cars imitating prestige marques. Not a mixture that I would expect from a senior general in Europe. He kindly gave me a lift back to the
hotel, therefore saving me from another taxi experience and its associated propositions.

By this time my cold was really getting me down and, as it was not too late in the day, I asked
reception for directions to the nearest pharmacy to see if I could buy some medicine to at least
improve my symptoms. It was good to learn that the hotel had a clinic of its own, but at the same
time I was quite alarmed when I was told with great insistence that it would be better if the nurse
came to see me in my bedroom. After my experiences outside I was getting paranoid about everybody's intentions and after a lot of insisting from reception and declining on my part, I was eventually told where the clinic was. The pleasant and efficient nurse in the clinic gave me some
medicine to clear my cold, together with the assurance that I wouldn't suffer from side effects.

That evening was spent in a fairly relaxed manner without the constant pressure of being
rushed by my tight schedule. I even had time to allow my curiosity to take me outside the hotel

to have a closer look at the waves of humanity sweeping past along the wide avenues. Unfortunately I was much too conspicuous in my flying suit and captain gold bars to be able to do this for more than a few minutes before the inevitable pimps discovered me and started again on the hard-sell trail. That's when I was sure they couldn't understand the word NO. The temptation of further explanation by means of a fist in the mouth was too great for me to stay outside any longer!

There was plenty of time to look up the weather forecasts on the internet and what I could see appeared promising. There were a number of tropical storms to the immediate south and south-east of Manila, but my track to the island of Guam would remain clear of any significant weather well past the window of time with which I was concerned. The fantastic number of emails from people all over the world with encouraging messages continued to be a great boost to morale: I hope I was able to answer everybody adequately. Some of these messages were coming from Abilene in Texas, where the local EAA Chapter (Experimental Aircraft Association sub-division) members were keen for me to stop at their airfield on my way through. Even though this was not part of my original plan, they sent me such a tempting invitation with offers of food and fuel, that in the face of such genuine enthusiasm I had to accept.

My cold symptoms were not easing off, but twelve hours probably wasn't long enough for the medication to take effect. I did continue to take it easy for most of the morning before having to go to the airport to see how Joy was progressing with my multifaceted clearances. To occupy my time, I went up and down a few times from my floor to the business room on the ground floor to print forecasts and charts from my software. Doing this I became aware of a number of very young local girls on their own using the lift to a variety of floors. These girls made an impression on me in a number of ways: they were terribly young and decidedly minor; they clearly were not staying at the hotel or staff members; most were obviously scared witless; and they all were dressed in wholly unsuitable cheap dresses. It then dawned on me that they had to be the girls that the pimps outside were sending directly to their customer's rooms. This realisation shocked me beyond any anticipation and their sad and scared expressions will remain with me forever. I felt a great urge to 'throw a wobbly' and create a huge scandal, but self-preservation prevailed and it was obvious, even to me, that the only consequence of note from that sort of action would be to get me into serious trouble. However the realisation of how low human misery can slump to was and remains terribly depressing. If nobody does anything at all, this will go on forever and thousands of young lives will continue to be cruelly damaged by the perverse lust of some and the greed of others. I would like to think that reporting these facts might help a little, but I fear it will not be enough.

My brushes with the seedy side of life did affect me quite badly and only looking back at it from a long way away, both in terms of time and distance, am I able to put the whole of the 'Manila experience' into context. I also became aware that my own state of health, as well as having made my journey much more difficult than necessary, clearly contributed to making the whole episode feel particularly dark. As an illustration of this distortion and at a much more trivial level, there were the taxi fares – normally I am quite good at being aware of local currency values and in Manila I simply wasn't. The taxi fares about which I got so heated up and which varied from 50 to 600 pesos, can actually be converted as ranging from US$1 to US$12 (under £6.50)! Although it doesn't remove the underhanded way of how some taxi drivers dealt with it, the actual sums involved were simply not an issue.

The afternoon of that day didn't get much better. Apart from further dealings with taxi drivers, the good news of Joy arranging a satisfactory outcome for my arrival in Guam with one of the handling agents in the US territory was heavily counteracted by the massive bill with which I was presented. The charges for landing, parking, navigation and tax came to over

US$2,000/£1,080 – and that will be cash, thank you. To say I was taken by surprise would be an understatement the size of the Pacific. However at least I was ready to leave and that felt good.

The rest of the day was spent refuelling, filing the flight plan, checking the weather on the internet and having a last meal in the oriental restaurant of the hotel. After a few hours sleep, I woke up feeling a lot better than of late and thought that it would be worth paying the 600 pesos and go to the airport in a hotel taxi without the usual hassle with the driver. I had mixed success: the girl driver was polite and impeccably turned out but didn't know the way. After a bit of wandering around, calling at some other airport access gates, we eventually got the necessary directions from a helpful passerby and found our way – taxis in Manila were certainly an experience not to be forgotten.

A lot of delays ensued in obtaining my weather files and I was finally informed that the forecast could only be delivered to me after I had cleared customs on the same apron as before. This reluctance to deliver was most odd as the lack of this vital information makes the planning of routes nonsensical. In fact it made the 'go-no-go' decision plain impossible. Almost as odd as customs being able to drive to a remote dark apron, but not to a perfectly well-lit hangar!

As nobody was going to do anything sensible, I ended up taxiing to the apron and waiting for somebody to come and clear the flight for customs and immigration purposes. Eventually a car did turn up with a few scruffy characters in civilian clothes and after a couple of inane questions they left without a word. Having assumed I had been cleared by customs, I waited in vain for the weather report. A radio call to the tower asking for the promised weather forecast was rewarded with an offer of the local TAF (terminal aerodrome forecast). I must say I didn't react well to that and apart from pointing out that I couldn't care less what the weather was going to do in Manila, a few sharp words ensued to the effect that an aviation forecast for the flight was needed – NOW! Eventually they promised to send somebody with the necessary documents and an individual turned up in a car with a bundle of A4 sized papers. The messenger dashed off and it soon became clear that the reason for his astonishingly hurried departure was because the forecasts were solely concerned with mud slides and tides in the Philippines and he clearly didn't wish to be around when I found that out. For a moment I felt a blinding fury, but I had studied the weather on the internet and what was really important to me was to get away. So I went ahead – goodbye Manila!

Chapter 10
MANILA TO GUAM

The take-off from Manila at sunrise catapulted me from the unfortunate experiences of that airport into a fantastic viewing position over the Philippines. The early morning light, the mist in the valleys and the rugged hills revealed a land of great beauty. This spectacle was shouting at me that there was a lot more to this country than the picture I had formed based on my own experiences in its capital. And that beauty was not only confined to the thirty-five miles across the big island, the small islands immediately to the east were just as fascinating. Of course I only had the opportunity to see these views because I had been delayed so long in Manila, had my departure gone according to plan I would have been crossing the country at night.

Above: Leaving Manila
Opposite: The mighty Pacific

HF communications with Manila were very difficult and before I was out of their zone I tried the Guam frequencies. The reply came loud and clear. I never thought I could have been so pleased to hear an American accent and I certainly was glad to be able to understand and be understood without constant repetition. I was, however, astounded by their call-sign and it took a few exchanges to really be sure of it: San Francisco! At first I wondered if there was another San Francisco anywhere around there, which of course there wasn't, then just marvelled at being able to talk to them as the distance involved was over 6,000nm (11,100km). Later on in Guam I learned that they had a relay station there, so maybe it wasn't so utterly astonishing, but it felt so at the time.

Once the sun rose sufficiently to lose its early morning softness, the overwhelming intensity of blue from the sea was complemented by the matching strong blue of the sky. This image was further enriched by the radiant exploding white of scattered CBs, providing me with the most spectacular welcome to the Pacific proper. This was it, the real thing, by far the biggest body of water on earth and, all going well, I would be overflying it for some sixty hours.

It is interesting to note that the total area occupied by the Pacific Ocean is greater than the combined areas of all the other oceans and vastly larger than all the land masses together, even if Australia was counted twice. Realising I had started to cross this vastness in a single-engined aircraft was not something that could be taken lightly.

While reviewing my experiences in Manila, I was not too sure of the effect my gold bar captain epaulettes had on other people and, what's more, on me. They may well have facilitated some processes in the course of this journey, but they also created what I thought was a neo-colonialist deference that I didn't like and might have jacked up some prices to boot. Although they did represent my capacity of pilot-in-command, I don't think my crew needed reminding of my status. Philly the mascot never hinted at mutiny or even muttered a disrespectful word! So I decided to remove them from my shoulders and they ended up in a pocket of the flying suit for the remainder of the journey. I felt much happier for that.

The actual flight was progressing well enough with the isolated CBs obligingly not interfering with my track. The traffic heard on the radio was fairly light and consisted mostly of airliners on the Australia-to-Asia and Australia-to-America tracks. Traffic on the sea was a lot less busy than on the way to Manila, where I had crossed one of the busiest shipping lanes in the world. This lack of human presence was, I suppose, the simple consequence of crossing that vastness of water.

Although the little headwind was barely slowing G-RV's progress, the distance of nearly 1,400nm (2,600km) made this leg the third longest so far. A good check on all the navigation and fuel usage was particularly important as the really long legs were now only one flying day ahead, and I simply had to have all performance parameters carefully quantified.

After I had flown about two thirds of the distance to Guam, I became seriously concerned about my difficulty in carrying out basic fuel calculations; this was scary. Despite the actual calculations being straightforward enough and required using an ordinary pocket electronic calculator as opposed to some sophisticated piece of equipment, my various results were either ridiculously wrong or they simply weren't achieving the same figure twice. This greatly worried me as it was clear that my brain was becoming very woolly, putting into serious doubt my ability to deal with the rest of the flight and carry out a decent landing at the end of it. The only explanation I could come up with for this impairment was the effects of the bronchial infection that had plagued me throughout this flight, despite its symptoms appearing considerably better since my medication in Manila. Of course I was also having doubts about the supposed lack of side effects from that medication, but what to do about it was less clear. For the lack of an obvious alternative, I just carried on the best I could and if things hadn't improved by the time the arrival at Guam was imminent (assuming I was going to find it!), I would go for a good dose of caffeine and hope for the best. Eventually, a snack of cereal bars, some great tasting fresh fruit and a long drink of water made me feel a lot better and by the time I was in VHF contact with the military Guam ATC, I felt quite happy to carry on with the approach and landing.

Philly spots Guam through the clouds

One significant difference from flying around Guam and the flying I had done before was that the altimeter pressure settings are expressed in inches of mercury instead of milibars as it is almost everywhere else. This is because Guam is an American territory and America hasn't gone metric. These settings are a critical piece of information for flights and especially so for the landing phase. To get around that problem Jill had emailed me a conversion table, but it must be said that it was a close call – I only remembered that I needed it in Manila.

From my research into the climate in the Pacific region, I was aware that its islands very often have cumulus clouds right above them and Guam in particular, so much so that cloud often completely obscures the whole island. This phenomenon has been known since the dawn of time and well before Europeans even knew about the existence of the Pacific. It allowed ancient navigators to locate unknown islands long before land could be sighted. On this occasion however, although cloud was present, I still could see the coast well before I got to the overhead and that allowed me to have a good look at the layout of the island. The problem was that this became too much of a distraction and while I was busy peering at Guam, I found myself once again too high and too close to the airfield. A quick call to ATC established that they were expecting me to descend at 'my discretion', so it was a case of another frantic dive onto the runway and into the care of US 'officialdom'.

The total time for the flight was ten hours and six minutes for a distance of 1,385nm (2,565km) giving a speed of 137.13kt (254kmh), not bad considering the headwind and the low power settings I had been using.

Once the aircraft was safely tied down on the handler's apron, I was taken to the main airport building to clear customs, security and immigration. The civilian airport (as opposed to the military one a little further north, which looked remarkably similar) is huge and so is its terminal, due to the large numbers of mainly Japanese tourists visiting the island. Apparently a great percentage of these Japanese are honeymooning couples, which is a pleasant change from the days of their presence on the island during the 1940s!

If there was any room for doubt as to whom Guam might belong, once confronted with the security/immigration/customs officials, that doubt would completely evaporate. There was an all-American show of attitudes and prejudices towards foreigners and the security checks to enter the island with metal detectors and luggage searches were tighter than the checks that can be expected when boarding the average airliner. I did wonder if they were worried that I was going to highjack the whole island! Immigration checks were most meticulous with camera shots and finger prints, although the actual people carrying it out were pleasant enough. The futility of it all bordered (pun intended) on the ridiculous.

Once cleared of bureaucracy, I went back to the handler's office where I started to have doubts about their efficiency as it wasn't clear when they could actually refuel the aircraft. As I was somewhat tired and still concerned about my mental arithmetic problems, I decided to have a full night's sleep and refuel the following day before my next flight to Bonriki.

The handler's ramp manager, Andrew, booked me into a local Days Inn, part of a well-known budget American hotel chain. The hotel provided their free shuttle from the airport and once I had settled in, the manager gave me a lift to the local twenty-four hour diner two blocks away, because the hotel didn't have restaurant facilities. Being in this very American diner, full of what was possibly a fair cross-section of the island's inhabitants, provided a great people-watching opportunity as well as some excellent and inexpensive food. It was here I discovered and greatly enjoyed Maui-Maui fish. Admittedly not having any 'proper' food for the last day or so would probably have made the paper tablecloth quite edible!

Despite people using mobile phones, as people do everywhere in the world, and despite the building of the mobile telephone company right opposite the hotel, my phone didn't work here as it would appear that having only two frequency bands was not sufficient in Guam. Once more the use of the satellite phone was tried with no more success than on previous occasions – it just held long enough to let Jill know the hotel phone number and my room number so that she could call me back on the landline. Ringing home was highlighting the time difference between UTC (GMT to most of us) and local time as by now I was ten hours ahead of England. This time difference was much more obvious now that it covered two different calendar days, my breakfast time coinciding with late evening of the previous day in England. I know a lot of people will have experienced this when talking to relatives and friends in faraway parts of the world, but when this time difference keeps changing on a daily basis, it can be confusing.

The Days Inn provided all rooms with internet access and this allowed me to catch up with my messages and to study what the weather would be like for my next flight. This was going to cover 1,833nm (3,395km) to Bonriki in Tarawa, capital of the Kiribati Islands (once known as Gilbert Islands) and the longest leg so far. I couldn't ignore the fact that Tarawa was 1° 20′ north, practically on the equator and therefore subject to the particular climatic conditions of this zone.

There is a permanent weather system in the tropics with thunderstorms and general bad weather, constituting a sort of belt around the Earth's midriff and called the inter-tropical convergence zone (ITCZ). It was reasonable to expect this in the southern hemisphere at that time of the year, however I didn't feel I could be too certain. Another critical aspect of this flight was that I had to be on the ground in Bonriki before sunset as there are no lights at all on the runway, so a start from Guam at 1.00 a.m. local time was essential.

Breakfast was not the strong point of this hotel chain, but at least I was refreshed by a reasonable sleep, aided by the air conditioner and feeling pretty much recovered from my cold. The first task was to go to a bank to change some traveller's cheques to balance out the ravages of the fees in Manila. What should have been a nice straightforward task became an almost impossible one as no bank was going to do this for me unless I had an account with them. Having queued for ages in three banks only tripled my frustration. While in town, I took the opportunity to go to a Korean supermarket and bought drinks and fresh fruit, which would nicely enhance the onboard menu.

Walking around Guam revealed the strong American identity and a happy and friendly population. In fact the island had a nice feel of 'small town America', complete with a much publicised wish to become a new state and a very large number of hot-rods and custom cars wherever you went. I wouldn't have been surprised if I had seen the Dukes of Hazzard coming from around a corner!

Relating my money changing difficulties to the hotel's manager, she assured me that it wouldn't be a problem at the airport terminal and gave me a lift there in the afternoon. I found the airport buzzing with activity and I changed my traveller's cheques without any problem. With cash in my pockets, I went across to the handling agents where I actually saw the fuel drums and organised the refuelling, which eventually took place later in the evening. I chose to do it then so that I wouldn't lose too much capacity by the fuel contracting with the change in temperature at night fall, but not so late that those who were going to actually carry out the refuelling had gone home. Quite a number of people were necessary to manhandle the fuel drums out of their storage, drive the fork lift truck and pump the fuel manually. The available helpers were quite young and possibly military personnel doing a bit of moonlighting. Their astonishment at my flight through the Middle East and overflying the Gulf placed me on a very high pedestal in their eyes, both amusing at a personal level and concerning as an expression of a national view.

Both before and after refuelling, I found myself going between the aircraft and the handler's office to try to get my aviation weather forecasts. As this office is not airside, there was a convenient gate in the fence which was completely unsupervised by the authorities. After the ridiculous screening of the previous day this was simply amazing – one day I couldn't take a penknife through the terminal onto the island, but the following day there was nothing to stop me (if I was so inclined) to go back to the aircraft and bring out enough explosives (if there were any in there) to send the airport into orbit! Splendid logic…

The likelihood of obtaining an aviation weather forecast wasn't looking good. Even the military air base appeared to have little information for the distances, direction and altitude I required, and I was rather surprised that in 2006 there were still so many difficulties in acquiring this data. The problem was, of course, the vastness of the Pacific, making observation stations around there pretty bit thin on the ground – or water, actually. Total fees came to US$580/£313, exclusive of fuel at $1.60/£0.86 per litre.

After a final study of weather charts on the internet, I went back for another early dinner at Danny's Diner. This time I thought I wouldn't be so adventurous with my food and went for a steak. This decision was influenced by reading the opinions of another 'Earthrounder' like myself, and I suppose it must reduce the risk of any gastric incident, something too horrendous to contemplate within the confines of the cockpit of an RV-6.[9]

Whilst enjoying my food and thinking idly about recent events, a possible reason for my woolly brain became apparent. I had been flying at an indicated FL095 (9,500ft) and with an outside temperature of 17°C, this equated to an altitude density of just over 12,000ft, high enough to show up signs of oxygen starvation. I have had occasion to learn since then that pressure alone has a bearing on the breathing process, but at the time it was a 'Eureka' moment.

This altitude density coupled with my remaining cold symptoms was more than enough to create the kind of problems I had experienced, something I was going to have to be particularly observant about from now on, despite feeling fully recovered from my cold. I was going to have to think of a self-diagnostic to this type of condition, as this situation is not unlike being drunk – i.e. the last one to be aware of the situation is the actual individual. Eventually I decided that the simplest solution would be to regularly test myself by a series of mental arithmetic operations followed by its reversal, so I should return to the initial figure generated by a reasonably random process.

Quite pleased with myself for discovering a reason for my partial incapacitation during the previous flight, I decided it was time to get a little sleep before my departure to Bonriki in Tarawa.

Chapter 11
GUAM TO TARAWA

Despite getting up just before midnight local time, I felt better rested than I had for a long time, no doubt through having recovered from my chest infection and feeling more relaxed having found the reason for the woolly brain episode. After a midnight breakfast from the provisions of my earlier shopping trip, I was given a lift to the airport by the hotel's duty manager after settling the bill for a reasonable US$122/£66 for the two nights.

No weather forecast had materialised for my route to Tarawa, but as I had spent so much time staring at weather information from the internet, I was not feeling too concerned. After a pre-flight check by the lights of the apron and my small Maglite torch, I took off into an overcast sky to start the longest leg so far, an estimated thirteen-and-a-half hours to cover 1,833nm (3,395km).

HF communications were quite difficult to start with and there were many towering cumulus with a lot of static electricity, although I didn't see any lightning strikes. Static and water from these clouds sometimes improved radio communications, but occasionally made them unusable, and this was always impossible to predict. What all this static electricity did provide was a most spectacular *son et lumière* show with sparks actually inside the cockpit! These sparks were fat and blue, not unlike those from an engine spark plug and I had four separate tracks of lightning right in front me, jumping between an internal metal reinforcement at the forward end of the canopy and the glare shield over the instruments. The radio interference from these sparks was making sure that not only could I see them, but I also had to hear them. The fact that I was sitting next to two fuel tanks containing 240 litres of Avgas one inch to my right and big blue sparks one foot in front of me gave that extra touch of unwanted excitement.

As with everything in aviation, the need to prioritise is essential, as the maxim, 'aviate, navigate, communicate', so well illustrates. No matter what else is going on those priorities have to be followed and the task of aviating is the first and overriding consideration. So sparks or no sparks, I simply had to concentrate on the necessary tasks and carry them out to the best of my ability. On the positive side, I was aware that the fuel tanks have no vents to the inside of the aircraft, so the possibility of a 'big bang' was not likely – on the other hand, if it had actually happened and if there had been a passing ship 10,000ft below, they would have been treated to a spectacular fireworks display.

As this was not only the longest leg so far, but also prior to the longest single flight of the whole adventure, I had to give particular attention to all aspects of maximising my range. Speed had to be sacrificed for endurance and the leaning of the fuel mixture had to be monitored and adjusted with great precision. However, speed couldn't be completely ignored as I could not forget the lack of runway lights in Bonriki airport, I had to make sure that I arrived there in daylight.

Above: Sunrise over the Pacific with clouds full of
  static electricity
Middle: Mysterious Pohnpei ahead
Bottom: Mokil

The long-awaited sunrise over the Pacific was stupendously spectacular and the combination of tropical dawn colours with the magnificent large and somewhat intimidating cumulus was a view I will never forget. This was replaced by a display of two intense and distinct blues from sky and sea contrasting with the white fluffy fair weather cumulus well below my cruising level, the most gorgeous surroundings for the solo pilot. The privilege of being in my own small aircraft enveloped by all that beauty, seemingly for me and me alone for as far as I could see, hour after hour, is a pleasure that few humans have been able to enjoy, but is one of the great experiences of life. It brings a degree of involvement with nature that, along with an implied clear statement of human frailty, excludes everything else as mere distractions.

After 900nm (1,670km) I was overhead Pohnpei, one of the most intriguing islands in the world. Apart from its sheer natural beauty, eight centuries ago Pohnpei was the home of an ancient civilisation that left a legacy of a lost city made from huge stone blocks without any explanation for its construction or demise. Whilst overflying its runway I made a few calls on the published frequency to wish them a good day, but got no reply. With high peaks of over 2,000ft and some sixteen miles (26km) across, it looked larger than I expected and definitely the sort of place requiring a few days to enjoy. But I had records to chase, so I had to forget that idea.

Pohnpei was the first and largest of four islands I was going to overfly within the space of 300nm (555km) and they provided a safety net if things were to go wrong, particularly as two of them were marked as having runways, but no published availability of Avgas.

Mokil, the second island of that chain, was beautiful and very low. I thought it looked far too small to support a human settlement, but I was wrong, now I know there are about 300 people living there and they even have their own language.

The third island, Pingelap, was tiny and, from where I saw it, just about the most perfect vision of paradise on earth. I have learnt since that this island is known as the island of the colour-blind due to an exceptionally high incidence of a rare and total colour blindness condition in the indigenous population. Despite my aeronautical information telling me it didn't have an airfield it certainly did have a very obvious runway. It was even more difficult to resist the temptation of a quick visit, but as I had told myself before, there were records to try and break.

The last of these islands, Kosrae, was the other which also had a runway and the whole place looked like a scaled-down version of Pohnpei. It had the same type of archaeological remains as the bigger island. It would have been a fascinating and rewarding quest to unlock its secrets, but one must get a lot lower – and slower – than I did! Again I called but nobody answered.

As a further pleasure, I was able to supplement my usual diet of cereal bars and mineral water with the fresh fruit I had bought in Guam, a most welcome addition to my meals and I made a mental note to try very hard to buy it whenever possible.

Above: The runway in Pingelap

After Kosrae I had about 600nm (1,110km) to run to Bonriki without any further islands. This was looking like an easy run without any unforeseen problems but, as usual when I had similar thoughts, I was wrong. Somewhere half-way between Kosrae and Bonriki I met a great wall of CBs. Initially I was not too sure what it was, but eventually had to come to the conclusion that, despite being in the wrong hemisphere, I had found the ITCZ. This was both scary and exhilarating. The barrier made by these very large and tall clouds was very deep. However I was lucky to find narrow gaps of clear air separating them and I was able to slalom between them with the most thrilling high bank turns between walls of pure white. As I always found a gap after coming around each narrow curving corridor, the seriously scary part of actually entering a CB never actually took place. After around thirty minutes of this extraordinary experience, I came out of the zone having to finish the last part by climbing to an indicated 12,000ft for short periods and with much mental arithmetic testing in-between. I am glad to report that the grey cells passed the tests.

South of the ITCZ I found a lot more clouds than before and they were split into two layers, one layer of scattered alto-cumulus higher than my level and a broken layer of cumulus below me. Oddly enough, it was around here that I experienced an episode of high anxiety. It was the sort of anxiety that gives clammy hands, and a feeling with which I am not accustomed so it was the source of great discomfort. This tension came about for a number of reasons: first of all the fuel gauges were reading much lower than before; the safety bolt hole of the last island was well behind me and on the other side of the ITCZ; and finally the cloud cover underneath me would prevent spotting a small island at anything more than a very short distance. Trying to rationalise these feelings was not easy, but essential. So the first thing I had to analyse was the fuel situation.

Of course it was reading lower than in the previous flights, after all this was the longest leg so far, so I would have used more fuel. But what would happen on the next leg? This was going to be even longer! Telling myself that I could reach Bonriki and then assess the situation afterwards didn't help that much. Having the safety of the last island to land on if needs be was easier to deal with. After all this was the leg where I had the luxury of islands with runways as a possible diversion in an emergency. None of the other overseas legs had that possibility, so I came to the conclusion that this was my mind trying to cling onto a 'safety blanket' and, relative to previous flights, there was nothing new about this situation. Finally, the possibility of not being able to spot an island other than on the overhead was making me question whether I should have installed an automatic direction finder (ADF). ADF is a radio navigation aid and at that point it would have given me the only instrument alternative to the GPS.

Fortunately the GPS was functioning perfectly and if it was going to fail on me, I felt moderately happy to implement the deliberate error navigation technique devised by Sir Francis Chichester. He utilized 'off-course navigation', to create a deliberate error to one side of the track, therefore ensuring that the aiming point would always be on the opposite side. This technique was used extensively by the RAF in World War II so I felt in good hands. Had that happened, I knew I could also increase my visibility range at the surface by descending below the lowest cloud layer. These considerations allowed me to keep the worst of that anxiety at bay.

San Francisco radio was a reliable companion, they gave me the impression they were looking after the flight. This was particularly well-demonstrated when crossing the boundary into the Fiji area and I was handed on to Nandi radio, as the new operator didn't seem too bothered about replying to my call, possibly because of my weak signal. San Francisco, clearly listening to my unanswered calls, gave him a sharp verbal push and communications with Nandi from then on became quite smooth.

The communications with Bonriki didn't start too well: HF calls were not answered at all and I only established a useful VHF exchange at about 40nm (74km), as the initial contact some 60nm (110km) away didn't achieve anything. It quickly became clear that nobody was expecting me – didn't anybody there read the flight plans? The radio call asking me the purpose of my visit to Kiribati with an undertone of complete surprise as to why anybody would want to go there was certainly unusual. My reply stating, "to land", didn't enlighten and was not fully appreciated.

Tarawa, the island on which Bonriki is built, finally appeared to my right. It was some seventeen miles (29km) long and very narrow, no more than half a mile (1km) wide, and I had the airport in sight with some 28nm (45km) to go. A little further on, the tower gave me a weather report with a visibility of 5km and a cloud base of 1,600ft, which sounded quite puzzling as I could clearly see it was several times greater than stated.

After the tower operator asked me for range when I was just a quarter of a mile away and with the landing light on, I arrived at a runway in good condition and parked on the apron next to a very dilapidated Piper Aztec twin-engined aircraft, the only other light aircraft to be seen anywhere. Climbing out of the aircraft after a flight of fourteen hours and twenty-three minutes into a very hot end of the day (evenings are a bit difficult to define in the tropics) gave a much appreciated opportunity to straighten myself out. In that flight I had covered 1,833nm (3,395km) at an average of 127.74kt (236.6kmh) with, despite my earlier worries, an excellent reserve of fuel.

Whilst trying to get myself upright and mobile, a group of over twenty young children with beaming faces came climbing onto the fence immediately behind the aircraft asking all the obvious questions. My arrival was clearly a big event around there. A little later on, a local chap who spoke quite good English, just as curious as his younger country fellows, was clearly preoccupied with my ethnic origin. When I told him I was from England his reaction was to ask, clearly concerned, if I was, "a pure blood Englisher". From this I presumed that race is an important factor in Tarawa. In such a small place it probably is important to distinguish between those from within and those

Dilapidated yet amazing Piper Aztec in Bonriki

from outside. Whatever his reasons, I was quite sure that there was no malice in his ethnic considerations.

The female controller and only occupier of the tower, Kauna, came down to welcome me to Kiribati, pronounced 'Kiribatis'. This is the country that Tarawa belongs to and has its capital in Betio, the furthermost western point of this island. She was occupied making sure I would see all the officials I had to before leaving the airport. When pressed about calling Nandi to close my flight plan, she was rather unhappy at the prospect of climbing back up the tower to telephone Fiji, insisting instead that the following day would be perfectly adequate to do that. As one of the main points of a flight plan is to initiate search and rescue if an aircraft doesn't arrive at its destination, I didn't really want to be presented with the bill for such an operation once the authorities discovered I had arrived safely and hadn't bothered to close the flight plan. As my normal cell phone didn't work in Tarawa, this was the one occasion where the satellite telephone did earn its keep, working long enough to close the flight plan and even tell Jill I had arrived safely. With the cost of hiring the satellite phone equipment at £1,000, this might have been the one occasion where it could be felt as good value – at least compared with the cost of a search and rescue operation in that oceanic vastness.

As Bonriki doesn't normally stock Avgas, the next thing was to find the fuel that had been shipped for me to Bonriki from Christmas Island, which had been confirmed as accomplished a few weeks before I had left England. Kauna led me into the refuelling building and the guy there denied any knowledge of my fuel or even any recollection of the name of the chap with whom I had been in contact about the shipment. I absolutely refused to panic and, after much insistence, he did admit that there might be another fuel company somewhere else. It eventually turned out it was right next door to him! Unfortunately there was nobody around to solve the issue, so I would have to wait for the following day to learn anymore about my fuel.

All there was left to do was to wait until the two separate officials from immigration and customs were located and decided to come and see me. Promises that I wouldn't swim away leaving the aircraft there didn't inspire anybody in the little group keeping me company (consisting of Kauna, a policeman and a member of airport security) to allow me to leave for the hotel.

Despite having previously read that the fence around the airport had a few holes, it was still astonishing to see that there were people, vehicles and animals wandering in and out of it – including onto the runway. It was certainly very different from the unbelievably strict security of most other airports.

It was dark by the time the first official appeared, a very giggly immigration officer who relieved me of US$40/£22 in exchange for a scribbled note on the back of a scrap of paper found in a drawer. She wasn't going to let me go to the hotel either, not until the customs man turned up to clear my arrival. The only reason I just didn't go to sleep on the check-in counter was her lively and incessant chatter. Having established all my background and family, she was absolutely insistent that I would have to take my daughter a Kiribati shirt that she was going to make in time for my departure the following night. As there was no way she was taking no for an answer and had announced she was going to come and see me at the hotel to stamp my passport once more and take the opportunity to give me the shirt, I felt obliged to invite her to dinner, after all it was the polite thing to do.

Eventually the customs official appeared and showed a complete lack of interest in my flight, so I was at last allowed to leave the airport. The policeman gave me a lift to the Otintaai Hotel in the police SUV at 9.00 p.m., just in time for the last dinner orders. After a forgettable but appreciated meal, I finally slumped into bed an hour later enjoying the effective air conditioner and feeling rather tired. Understandably so, I had been on the go for the last twenty-two hours with over fourteen hours of flight.

Chapter 12
A LONG WAIT IN TARAWA

As soon as I stepped out of my air-conditioned room, the hot and humid conditions of the equator hit me like a boxing glove. I was now the furthest I could have been from home, as I was literally on the other side of the world. Any further travelling would now reduce the distance. Therefore the time difference was also the full twelve hours, so what to me was then nine in the morning of Sunday 12th March, was simultaneously nine in the evening of Saturday 11th March at home. A leisurely breakfast in the hotel restaurant overlooking the open lagoon was an excellent way to acclimatise and afterwards the owner was kind enough to arrange for a driver to take me to the airport.

When I got there the deserted apron was incredibly hot with no shade at all under the late morning sun. As I was obviously the only person around there, Noel Coward's song about 'mad dogs and Englishmen out in the midday sun' seemed a suitable tune to hum. As if to reinforce the point, the metal of the aircraft was too hot to touch with a bare hand and just about feasible with my flying gloves. The LCD display of the engine monitor was also suffering from the heat and had turned black all over. I was well aware that if it wasn't going to recover, this would constitute a serious problem. By covering the instrument panel with my reflective survival blanket and leaving the canopy partially opened, the display started to improve, but I wasn't at all G-happy with this situation and I was going to have to try very hard to get G-RV into the one and only hangar in the airfield.

However, despite these concerns, I just couldn't avoid being amazed by the Aztec parked next to me. This aircraft, obviously owned by a religious mission, had clearly been parked there a long time as demonstrated by its flat tyres and cracked and crazed windows. What made it quite unique was the 'artwork' on its tail: this consisted of a child-like painting of the planet Earth as seen from above the Pacific Ocean. There was the sea sprinkled with little sailing boats carrying what were possibly lost souls and an angel flying the said Aztec. Extraordinary!

Trying to appear sensible and avoid the association with mad dogs, I went to look for shelter in the tower, simultaneously looking for Kauna to get my record forms signed and to find out what was likely to be happening around there, if anything. From what I had seen during my unscheduled long wait at the airport the night before, the weekend is a serious period of rest and nothing happens much at all. Kauna wasn't in the tower; instead there were some young girls staffing the place who didn't give the impression that they were in control of the situation, and certainly didn't know anything about my flight. Their poor command of the English language and my ignorance of theirs didn't help. After a lot of discussion, or more accurately, two parallel discussions, they rang the Met Office in the capital Betio (they pronounced it 'Peso') and handed me the phone so I could talk directly to the guy on duty over there. After a frustrating conversation, it was obvious that no forecast was coming from there and I just had to accept his promise that they would provide me with one for my departure to Honolulu the following day. In the unlikely event that refuelling was going to happen quicker than that, I just would have to depart with whatever information I gathered from the internet, just as I had done in Guam.

Whilst in the tower, it looked as if the airport was starting to wake up and a Twin Otter aircraft began doing some circuits. Listening to the radios in the tower explained my problems communicating with it – the background noise and speech quality was absolutely dreadful. Although if that was a shortcoming of the equipment or the way it was set was open to debate. When they actually used the radio, the weather information passed onto a second arriving aircraft bared no resemblance to reality. Despite glorious weather all around, they were reporting exactly the same ridiculously low cloud and visibility information I was given upon my own arrival the day before. I wondered if this is what every aircraft was told when arriving there, irrespective of what is actually happening.

With the arrival of the second aircraft, which I believed was a Shorts Sherpa (unkindly nicknamed 'Shed'), the place became quite active and a fuel truck appeared, not in the colours of Air BP as per the fuel guy of the previous evening, but with KOIL written on its sides. This appeared promising and worthy of further investigation, so I quickly got myself to the apron in the midst of lots of activity with some people boarding the first aircraft, others disembarking the second one and the fuelling truck busy pouring Jet fuel.

The person clearly in charge of all this activity was the chief engineer of Air Kiribati and he introduced me to the KOIL refuelling chap. KOIL, as in Kiribati Oil, is the company representing Mobil-Exxon with whom I had arranged the transfer of fuel to the island before my departure. The refueller, one Francis Green, did know about the Avgas they had for me, but it was in Betio, not in the airport! Francis, the son of a passing English serviceman, confirmed my view of the Kiribati attitude towards the weekend – life is very quiet in Tarawa on a Sunday, but I was assured there would be no problem to refuel me on Monday but not a chance before then. I was baffled as to why the fuel should be at the opposite end of the island to the airport and in my annoyance, I felt it wouldn't take a genius to work out that an aircraft would be arriving at the airfield and not in a sea port in the middle of a town. However, this was one of those times when jumping up and down demanding results would produce no solutions whatsoever, so I thought I might as well resign myself to reality and accept that this is the way of life in Kiribati. I must admit I found this attitude in tune with its environment, even if it wasn't helping me much.

With the fuel situation well and truly out of my hands, I went to the Air Kiribati hangar to look for the chief engineer to try and arrange hangarage to protect G-RV from the searing heat. While waiting for him, I had a look around the place and I was told by one of his engineers that what I had thought were a DHC Twin Otter and a Shorts Sherpa, were in fact respectively a Chinese Harbin-Y12 and a Spanish CASA 212-200. Eventually I found the chief engineer in his office and he was most helpful and informative, although I am ashamed to say I have forgotten his name, so I hope he will forgive me. Despite having enough space under the wings of their aircraft, he had to clear it with Dennis, the operations manager, who apparently had set the fee for the hangarage at AUS$100 (the currency of the Kiribati Republic). Dennis actually turned out to be Denise and she was very enthusiastic about the flight, not only waiving the hangarage fee, but also making a personal contribution and adding her name as a sponsor on the wing.

As I was clearly going to be in Tarawa for a lot longer than anticipated, the engineer agreed to arrange a hire car for me that was to be delivered to the hotel later on. Whilst waiting for a

G-GDRV hiding from the sun

lift to the hotel, I tried the tower once again and this time Kauna was there so she signed my record forms and also faxed my flight plan to Nauru for my flight to Honolulu in the early hours of Tuesday morning.

After placing G-RV in the hangar it was cordoned off as Denise was concerned about its fuel tanks containing Avgas (their aircraft use Jet fuel which is much less ignitable) and I returned to the hotel, courtesy of a lift from the first officer of the Harbin Y-12.

Road traffic in Tarawa was fairly light and there was no possibility of taking a wrong turn as there is only one road. I saw a fair amount of very crowded mini-buses running at regular intervals as a seemingly efficient public transport. These minibuses made numerous stops along the well-paved road, despite the presence of many speed-bumps along its length.

All vehicles appeared to be of Japanese manufacture with the vast majority Toyotas, mostly imported second-hand, as seen all over south-east Asia. The hire car was delivered to me at the hotel. As expected it was a small Toyota but complete with air-conditioning, a valuable feature over there. On the subject of cars, I noticed during my travels to and from the airport that the scrapping of dead cars was simply a matter of leaving them by the roadside as a self-service of donor parts for their ailing siblings. Afterwards they were recycled becoming play centres for the local children. By all accounts cars appear to rust very quickly, as would be expected on such a small island by the equator.

As there was still a reasonable amount of daylight left, I had a look around the grounds of the hotel. It consisted of four or five buildings on a fairly large plot of land and provided reasonably comfortable accommodation, with access to the internet which I found most useful. A courtyard open to the sea, flanked by the restaurant and a games room, also had a splendid indigenous construction right by the shore. This was the sort of building I was to see in a few places around the island, possibly for community gatherings and ceremonies and it was totally built by traditional methods. Its structure consisted of bamboo canes of very large diameter (over eight inches) and palm tree trunks locked together by notches cut into them for the required joints and tied together with vegetable fibres, not a single nail or screw to be seen! The roof was made of palm tree leaves and ended low enough for me to have to stoop to enter this fabulous construction of some 40ft x 50ft and about 30ft high at the centre. It was completely devoid of walls and it had a stage at the eastern end. Taking advantage of a couple of chairs left there, I sat in this splendid building with the warm sea lapping the rocks a couple of feet in front of me with the backdrop of the northern part of Tarawa the other side of the lagoon – this was a great place to meditate.

Sitting there it was impossible not to be awe struck by the enormity of the Pacific Ocean. Looking straight out, the next main landmass was the eastern tip of Russia 3,600nm (6,670km) away. To the north-west there was Japan at 2,700nm (5,000km), to the north-east the USA at 4,100nm (7,600km) and somewhere behind me Australia 1,800nm (3,330km) away. Everything was of a mind-numbing scale, particularly if the person having these thoughts is there in his small single-engined aeroplane! Considerations of how I was going to make sure I had enough range to get to Hawaii and questioning the saneness of the whole project were soothed by the calm of my surroundings and the tranquillity of the lagoon. As the immigration lady had post-poned her visit, I was left to contemplate further the finer points of my next leg in the peace and quiet of dinner on my own.

After again unsuccessfully attempting to ring Jill on the satellite phone my frustration was further aggravated by the voice-activated land line – everything seemed to be conspiring to make communications incredibly difficult. This was already a difficult enough conversation, as on the one hand I wanted to share my thoughts with Jill and on the other hand I desperately wanted to shield her from my fears. I was acutely aware that one wish was incompatible with the other. Subtleties were totally lost by every other phrase consisting of, "say again".

Relaxing at my favourite building in a chair overlooking the lagoon went a long way to help contain my fears. At night the place was even more inspiring. The stars, a few lights from the northern part of Tarawa and the reflections from the water made it all look even more detached from the world of bustle and competitiveness from where I had come.

Monday morning started in a very sociable manner. The three, and only, westerners I had noticed the previous night introduced themselves and we had breakfast with animated conversation, an unusual event for a solo pilot. After my *faux pas* of asking them if they were Australians, I found they were from New Zealand and were there on a fact-finding mission about the effectiveness of the fight against leprosy, a major problem in some of the remote isles of the Pacific. John, a doctor with a long army career behind him, was heading the mission with Michael and Brian providing technical and logistical support for the project. They were all extensively travelled, they had all been to the most remote places in the world and they all had fascinating stories to tell. Their work sounded splendid by all accounts but, due to a lot of un-cooperative health officials in many places, it didn't sound to be an easy task.

After breakfast I went for a drive the length of the island. This was a great opportunity – after all, it's not everyday that a European can visit a remote Pacific island well away from the tourist-trodden paths. Simply buying petrol made the start of the journey pretty unusual when the petrol station is made entirely of coconut trees with the exception of the pump and fire extinguisher!

I drove along the road to the western end of the island, the most populated part of Tarawa. This island has a population of some 28,000 people and because of its size it is fairly densely inhabited. As well as being short of space, the land didn't seem to be very fertile and to a great extent, these islands have to rely on the help of other countries. I understand New Zealand is the biggest contributor. The housing I saw was largely basic and made of local natural materials. The people themselves didn't show signs of ill-health and gave an air of contentment with a good-natured demeanour. I thought they may well have a quality of life better than their modest surroundings might suggest.

Towards the western end there were quite a number of Christian missions from a variety of denominations. These missions were very easy to spot as they had by far the most substantial and elaborate buildings with a puzzling amount of security fences, iron railings and gates. Maybe the good word needs to be kept safe from the masses!

My attempts to find the maritime port were futile, I suspected that the access to it might have been hidden behind some gates in the industrial or warehouse area. I was quite disappointed as Tarawa is a well-known stop-over point for yachts crossing the Pacific, and it would have been fun to chat with people doing a similar journey to mine by different means.

The parliament building is in Betio and looked pleasantly airy and modern, which isn't surprising as Kiribati only became fully independent from Britain in 1979, making this country of islands spread over a vast area of the Pacific Ocean a very young nation indeed. Being a new

country does not mean it is devoid of history and the relics of the 1940s I found on the south coast of Betio were a testament to one of the darkest moments of the island and of the history of the Second World War. Tarawa was the scene of one of the bloodiest battles of the Pacific war, as the heavily-armed Japanese occupying forces in this strategically important position vainly defended their position from a much stronger American force. This battle was fought with great heroism and savagery from both sides with the American force taking the island despite a loss of just over 1,000 lives and some 3,000 injured. The Japanese contingent of 4,800 had only seventeen survivors. All this loss of life happened in just three days.

Nowadays, a couple of battle-damaged coastal defence guns and some concrete bunkers are all that is left for the casual observer. The amount and the type of damage done conveys to this day a sense of brutality that is a sad reflection of the human race. It is said that after the battle the American forces had to clear the devastation and death by bulldozing all remains into the ground and one only has to scratch the surface to come face to face with the reality of that battle.

Reeling from these thoughts, I drove over to the eastern end of the island to see what was happening at the airport.

Nothing! The fuel hadn't arrived. I would be lying if I said this surprised me, but I must admit I felt quite annoyed at the complete lack of action. Letting the weekend go by was one thing, but Monday was another matter and I certainly thought that it wasn't unreasonable to expect the fuel ordered especially for me to be actually delivered when needed. After all they had had several weeks in which to do it. After demanding in the strongest possible terms that the fuel had to be delivered before the end of the day, I actually believed Francis when he said it would be done

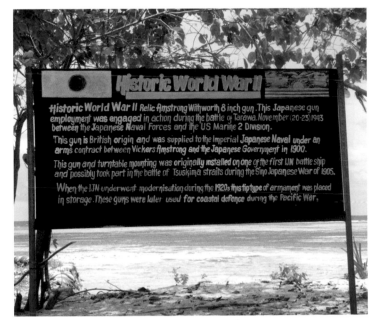

Top: A witness to the brutal battle of Tarawa and, *above*, a revealing notice

Going once more to the tower to try to get the weather forecast was not so promising. Another group of what I unkindly thought of as 'girlies', accompanied by an equal number of boys, rang the Met Office for me as the others had done the day before and, of course, the guy at the other end of the phone didn't have the weather forecast. My sense of humour had by then started to fail me and I launched into a dramatic explanation of how he would be personally responsible for my death if this was a result from his failure to carry out his job. I didn't know if that was going to produce any results but, as he sounded suitably guilty, I felt much better.

After popping back into the hotel for a quick late lunch, downloading the weather and printing my information from FlightStar, I felt that the weather was not going to give me any great problems. By then I was full of confidence about my abilities to interpret wind charts and I couldn't foresee any significant difficulties.

When I got back to the airport, the fuel had arrived – hooray! The euphoria was quickly dampened as, upon inspection, the drums were marked Avgas 100/130, with no mention of 100LL, which was the fuel I had ordered. The LL part of the fuel designator means low lead (low being relative to normal, but still very high compared with leaded Mogas) and as the fuel in the those drums had a higher content of lead, this could possibly result in problems with fouled sparking plugs. This situation was exacerbated as I needed to extend the range as much as possible, and therefore had to use very low power settings on this leg to Honolulu. A little uncertain of the whole thing, I decided to accept this fuel but, after placing the aircraft and the pick-up with the fuel drums in a suitable place to make the transfer, I noticed the very dirty hand pump with a split hose. The solution was for them to pump fuel into a clean bucket to wash the pump and if it all looked acceptable, start the actual refuelling. The fuel coming out of the pump eventually became clean, so with a helper holding together the split in the hose with his hands, G-RV was finally refuelled.

Refuelling Bonriki style

Once I got back to the hotel, the evening started full of telephone calls and visits. The immigration lady, who had arranged to come and stamp my passport, was the first to turn up and didn't appear to appreciate my efforts in having my documents ready for her down in reception, thereby saving her the trouble of going upstairs to see them and once again relieved me of a further US$40. She was most apologetic for not having been able to make the promised shirt and was absolutely determined that I would have a shirt for my daughter, no matter what I said, so she bought one from the hotel's display case! I couldn't completely suppress the unkind thought that I had just paid US$80 for a AUS$30 shirt, but I am sure I was wrong. Shortly after she left, the Civil Aviation chief rang concerned about my flight plan starting before dawn as the lack of airport lights and the possibility of animals on the runway wouldn't make it safe, although he put it a lot stronger than that. After a lot of discussion on how they wanted to ensure safety and security and my need to use as much of daylight as possible, we eventually agreed on a 5.00 a.m. start. Then, just as I going for dinner, the Met Officer came full of apologies and with a number of forecasts he had received from Honolulu. The threat of being made responsible for my impending death had obviously made an impression! Regrettably the forecasts were mainly concerned with the Kiribati islands and they were of little use to me. He did promise to fax any further weather forecasts to the hotel if there were any more to come, but nothing appeared before I left.

Dinner was a pleasant occasion with the New Zealand chaps, despite my attempt at jokes on the lines of the last supper and the last meal before the gallows. They were too kind and polite to entertain my black sense of humour, whatever they might have thought. They were in fact great at lifting my spirits and if the flight had depended on the amount of good wishes I received from them, there wouldn't be any problems at all.

Before paying the hotel for the three nights, meals and internet access as well as fresh sandwiches and bananas for the flight for a very reasonable total of AUS$395/£130, I spent a little time in my 'meditation den'. My anxieties about pushing the limits of my range if conditions strayed significantly from my estimates were causing a lot of plain fear, despite all my calculations favouring its successful completion. Logic was all very well, but it was my backside strapped to the aircraft and that does taint one's view! It is at times like this that you are reminded that courage is not the opposite of fear, courage is having fear and finding a way of overcoming it – not having fear is pathological. But courage wasn't easy to find. With that filling my thoughts it was time to try to have some sleep in the comfort of my air-conditioned room before setting off for the airport in the morning.

Chapter 13
TARAWA TO HONOLULU

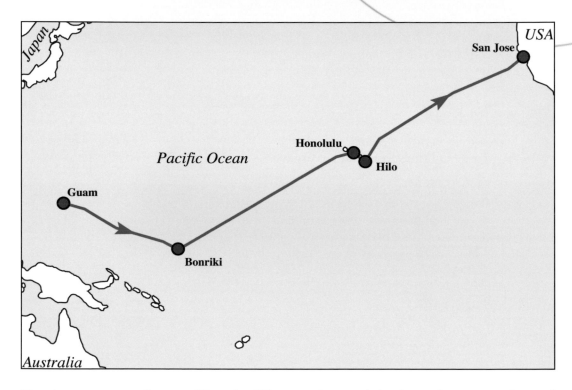

Heat is a permanent feature of Bonriki. Whenever I opened the door of my air-conditioned room I found the equatorial heat and humidity always waiting just outside the door to ambush me with its hot and sticky cloak. Leaving my hotel room for the last time in the middle of the night was no exception as at 4.00 a.m. the temperature was 28°C.

Nevertheless, although the weather was hot and sticky, it was not quite as unbearable as during the day. The position of such a small island in the middle of a warm ocean less than 100 miles from the equator is not enough to compensate for the absence of the immensely powerful tropical sun. Evidence of this drop in temperature became obvious when checking the fuel levels in the tanks – the five litres or so apparently missing hadn't just vanished, they were simply the consequence of fuel contraction through cooling.

The question of having my fuel tanks absolutely full or not was purely academic as there was nobody there to deliver it. It was not easy to remind myself that my often repeated calculations concluded I could accommodate that shortfall. Having to perform the final pre-flight check solely by the light of my pocket Maglite torch ensured my mind remained concentrated on the task in hand and away from the darker scenarios of starting my longest ever flight without having all fuel tanks brimming with Avgas.

Whilst finishing my pre-flight checks, I noticed the lights in the control tower were switched on, clearly proof that the airport was more efficient than I had thought. This obviously meant that somebody would be in the tower for the arranged 5.00 a.m. departure and able to initiate an emergency rescue if it was needed or, if it wasn't, to activate the flight plan (the preferred option!).

As I already knew, there were no more lights of any sort in the whole airport. So, with all my own lights switched on, I backtracked on runway 09 confirming that the bleaching effect of the tropical sun on the painted runway centreline made it of little use in the darkness and at speed.

Lining up with what I hoped was the centre of the runway, I couldn't help having a last moment evaluation of the situation. It was a pitch-black moonless night; there wasn't an obvious white centre line to guide me during the high speed ground run; my taxi light only shone up to around 50ft (15 metres) ahead of the aircraft. The landing light was shining uselessly at the stars while the tail was still on the ground; the large holes in the fence could allow people and animals to wander onto the runway and I was surrounded by 450lt of 100 Octane Avgas – what a combination!

Upon being told by the girl in the tower to, "take off at your discretion", I started my take-off roll by pushing the throttle smoothly all the way forward, accelerating briskly into the great blackness. For a short time I was being guided merely by the tyre markings of previous landing aircraft, then by not much more than my direction indicator gyro and a faint and roughly symmetric outline of tree silhouettes. My nerve gave up before reaching an acceptable speed to raise the tail and I forced the heavy tail up, thereby overloading the main gear – but at last I could see where I was going a little better. Fortunately the undercarriage coped with the abuse and after what seemed an eternity, I was able to take off. I was finally flying without having hit anything!

Settling into the climb, the overriding priority was to conserve fuel, especially after my agonising range anxieties throughout the last few days. I was now into my longest ever single flight of 2,072nm (3,837km) GC distance. For this flight I had estimated a duration of seventeen hours without any possible en-route alternatives – just sea all the way. Above everything else I had to reduce power, shallow the climb and lean the fuel mixture from the start, so this became a busy time balancing engine temperatures, power and fuel flow. Once the cruise level of FL095 was reached, it was a matter of reducing power to 55% of maximum and trimming the aircraft as effectively as possible. I had to bear in mind that this trimming also involved moving around the centre of gravity (its position is a critical factor of an aeroplane and must remain between finely defined limits) closer to its ideal performance position by carefully prioritising the fuel selection from the various tanks.

Day broke just as I was starting to feel that I had the aircraft nicely set up. Soon afterwards I arrived at my old friend the ITCZ and curiously enough this was quite a different experience from my previous meeting with the big curtain of storms. Somehow the ITCZ looked less active than on my way into Tarawa, most probably due to the earlier time of the day, therefore the sun would not have had so much time to inject too much energy into those towering clouds. Of course, having successfully crossed that awesome natural barrier before made a huge psychological difference. By way of moderating this optimism I was well aware that the aircraft was still very close to the maximum all-up weight, therefore enthusiastic high bank turns to slalom around scary CB clouds needed to be avoided.

HF radio communications were very difficult in the first few hours of the flight. Using the

VHF radio I managed to summon assistance from a Qantas airliner and later on from a New Zealand one to relay messages to ATC, thanks to their superior equipment and greater altitudes. Around mid-morning the HF situation became easier, allowing me to talk directly to Nandi and then to San Francisco without too much trouble.

One of the most 'exciting' parts of this flight was that conventional fuel calculations carried out in the early hours of this journey all gave the same ominous result: my destination was totally out of reach! This was not a series of mistakes – the calculations were quite correct and based on my performance up to that point. This was certainly not for the faint-hearted. But, of course, I did make it to my destination in Honolulu and not into the tabloid's headlines. It wasn't a miracle, this dramatic change of survival prospects was simply due to these calculations being based on the poor performance of the aeroplane whilst heavily-laden with fuel and my subsequent survival was greatly helped by the continuous improvement of that performance, by simply using it up. Being aware of this in theory was one thing, having the required faith to wait for the expected improvement was something else. My thoughts turned again to the prospect of a 'watery grave'...

Something I found all but irrelevant due to the enormity of the distances involved was establishing the point of no return (PNR) by the accepted formulae. The calculation of the PNR, as the name implies, determines where going back to the starting point is no longer a possibility, a highly desirable piece of information when crossing inhospitable terrain such as an ocean. Unfortunately the possible and unforecast variation of the winds over such a vast distance made calculations very difficult and the fact that Bonriki had no runway lights only made matters worse. Eventually I found that the only useful calculation of this kind was to use the data from the actual flight up to the point of calculation and work out by what margin I might or might not go back to my starting point in Bonriki in daylight – it was quite a momentous occasion when I knew that going back was no longer possible.

The Point of No Return (PNR), expressed in units of time, is calculated as:

PNR = (endurance x return speed) ÷ (return speed + outgoing speed)

One of the things I had very high on my 'to do list' of personal goals was to witness the passage of the date line and I really didn't want to miss the point where my track crossed that line. As Jules Verne made widely known in *Around the World in Eighty Days*, his Phileas Fogg character had a full day subtracted from local time when he crossed this line travelling eastbound and I still see this as an amazing event. The schoolboy in me was full of anticipation for the moment that Tuesday became Monday, today became yesterday. Dr Who here I come...

But I missed it! The actual point where I crossed the dateline coincided with a position-reporting point and I was so involved with the necessary radio communication that the actual magic moment passed me by. So instead of one instant being Tuesday and the next being Monday at the same time, it was Monday at the same time plus ten minutes – not the same thing at all.

From then on and for the rest of this adventure I was going to have to cope with a scrambled sense of all things relating to time. Before reaching the date line I was quite happy with the relationship between UTC and local time. It was easy to convert to UTC by subtracting the required and permanently variable amount of hours within my internal clock. After crossing the date line the calculation had to be reversed and I had to start adding hours to the local time, totally confusing the issue. For the remainder of this flight I was only able to report actual times by reading whatever my dual display watch was saying: it certainly didn't mean much to me anymore, they were just numbers.

Look at the scale in the lower left corner! The distance represents 400 nautical miles.

A little while after going directly from the furthermost eastern region of the globe to the furthermost western region, I was able to marvel at the graphic representation of the Pacific's vastness through the screen display of the GPS moving map. Even by zooming out so the width of the screen was representing around 3,000nm (5,500km) of the earth's surface, the only feature visible that wasn't the blue of the sea was (just) the Hawaiian archipelago, no other land whatsoever was visible.

The weather was turning out much as I had anticipated. There was a light 15kt (28kmh) headwind, it was beautifully smooth. There were no clouds above me, there was a scattering of small puffy cumulus clouds below my level and the very few towering clouds I saw were way out of my way. These were great conditions in which to be flying, a sort of aviators' nirvana.

But that didn't last long, in the middle of the afternoon the auto-pilot started to create a lazy shallow pitch oscillation to disturb that glorious flight. After timing its influence on speed, I realised the aircraft was descending (increasing in speed) of its own accord, followed by a similar period of climbing (decreasing speed). By remaining level, I calculated that the average speed was slightly higher. Holding the altitude manually I was able to improve the overall performance a little. This clearly was something to be investigated once on the ground.

The sandwiches and cute stubby bananas from Bonriki were a great treat. As I've said food was a very important part of this adventure by not only carrying out its primary function of providing energy, but by also providing stimulation of the senses and a distraction to the technical and emotional overload of flying solo for such a long time without a break. This overload was not necessarily a bad thing – this was the ultimate expression of the activity I love. Any comparison with a simple form of transport from A to B is completely irrelevant, here it is the journey itself that is important.

As the end of the day approached, I couldn't quite shake from my mind what I had read about flights from California to Hawaii: fourteen hours of bliss and two hours of hell! I was hoping that this description wouldn't apply to my approach from the south-west as everything was looking just right and, after all, I had checked several weather charts and by then felt I was a bit of a self-taught meteorological expert.

The sunset was of an indescribable beauty – the lowering sun over to the left gave the thickening cloud layer below me the most glorious tones of red and orange and the equally low full

Above: The moon risen above the red clouds
Opposite: Honolulu in the rain

moon to the right provided a fantastic contrast with an intensely calming pure white light. Once again in this journey I felt the most privileged person on earth – the whole spectacle appeared to be provided by Mother Nature for me and me alone. Apart from the romantic notion that I saw myself as the only spectator of this natural choreography, the fact is that I very probably *was* the only person for hundreds of miles. This communion of the aviator with nature without any outside interference is one of the most spiritual experiences to which I have been exposed. For a long-distance solo pilot, this is the pinnacle of flying and I fear the occasion was much greater than the description.

With around 250nm (460km) to go to Honolulu I was aware that I was heading into a warm frontal system with its associated bad weather and my previous self-elected status as a meteorological ace was being rapidly demolished. I hadn't spotted that bad weather from my wind charts! By now the eerie moonlight showing all the details of the ever-growing clouds beneath me was quickly disappearing behind an upper cloud layer and the total darkness that followed turned the canopy into a mirror, a concave mirror of continuously variable radius. This was presenting me with a grossly distorted reflection of myself and the instruments, despite having the cabin lights at their lowest level of brightness. It was a disorientating experience, particularly as by then I was being enthusiastically bounced around the sky by the weather. The solution, as always, was to focus on the instruments and ignore the view outside – not as easy as it might sound however. To those undergoing instrument flying training, just imagine the hood or curtains blocking the view from outside being distorting mirrors facing you.

I found myself being directed to contact Honolulu Center on VHF much earlier than I ex-

---

The VHF radio range between stations A and B is calculated as:

Radio range (nm) = $1.22 \sqrt{\text{elev. A}} + 1.22 \sqrt{\text{elev. B}}$
where elev. is the height of the concerned point in feet.
This a maximum figure in ideal conditions.

pected. I didn't really think this would work as I was nearly 200nm (370km) from Hawaii and at my level of 10,000ft altitude, I didn't expect to be able to talk to them at anything much further than 60nm (110km). To my surprise it did work and I could only assume that their aerials were atop one of the mountains. On the Big Island the highest point is nearly 14,000ft and if that's where they were sited, it would help the range of their transmitters no end.

However, what I could hear on that VHF frequency wasn't encouraging – there were a number of airliners being diverted around storm cells whilst on their approach to the islands and that certainly made me conscious of how small 'Romeo Victor' was! Following my call to ATC to remind them that I was flying an RV-6 and that I had no weather radar or de-icing equipment, their reassuring reply was that the worst of the weather was not towards my path and that they would guide me around any problems if required.

This bad weather, along with my northwards travel by some 20° of latitude, brought the outside temperature down to an indicated +2° C and I started to pick up a little ice on the leading edge of the wings. To improve the situation ATC cleared me down to 6,000ft and at that level the indicated outside temperature went up to +9° C, so I was able to relax a lot more. But not for long...

Once I was directed to a lower level as part of the approach to Honolulu International, I suddenly heard a loud folkloric ghostly noise of 'hooo…hooo' coming from outside the aircraft! This went on for a couple of minutes and then just as suddenly as it had started, it stopped. Gingerly trying the controls, I was satisfied that they all seemed to work correctly and that the aircraft was flying perfectly well, but I was left wondering what on earth could have caused that noise, or indeed what could have fallen off the aircraft to have stopped it. About ten minutes later the same noise returned, this time coming from the other, starboard, side. Being so clearly from the opposite side and towards the rear did however allow me to diagnose the nature of my fellow 'travelling ghost': it turned out to be the mylar strips, man-made flexible 25mm wide substances that improve aerodynamic efficiency at high speed. They are used to bridge the gaps between the fixed surfaces and the tail controls surfaces, and were being torn off in the rain. Their vibration in the airflow had caused the menacing noise – the noise was scary but the absence of these strips was not critical. I don't consider myself superstitious, but this certainly was intimidating.

Eventually, I was radar-vectored to the ILS of runway 4R visually following a Boeing 767 and in turn being followed by a Boeing 737. The final approach into Honolulu International Airport was an optical experience I am not likely to forget. The 767 had landed ahead, I could see the landing lights of the 737 just over my left shoulder and the most glorious light display opened up in front of me with the lights guiding the air traffic to the runway reflected by the  sea water and the shape of the city lit up just behind and around the airport. All this was complimented by the sight of Pearl Harbor to my left. What a spectacle.

The landing was easy enough, finding the exit onto the taxiway wasn't. The seat cushion had settled even more since Manila and my view to starboard was nil. This would have been an annoyance at the best of times, but with a 737 on short finals behind me, it was a very fraught moment for both pilots and ATC. Eventually a taxiway appeared and I ended up in a cargo terminal, from where a fuel bowser belonging to Air Services, my ground handlers in Hawaii led me to the correct parking space. By carrying out this long taxiing exercise I discovered that by slackening off my shoulder straps I could greatly improve my view of the outside and hopefully that would help me to avoid fraught times such as the one I had just suffered.

Upon parking as directed and shutting down, it felt good to have that crossing behind me. Total time airborne had been sixteen hours and eighteen minutes and I still had enough fuel left for around two-and-a-half hours of flight. The engine monitor was over-optimistically indicating I still had four hours endurance, but I decided against re-calibrating it – I knew its error and was happy to leave it at that.

Showing off a wet garland

"Aloha!" said the attractive girl putting the traditional garland of flowers around my neck – a totally unexpected but very stylish way to finish such a great flight.

My reception committee was headed by the garland-bearing young lady along with the fuel truck driver and a helper who timely and helpfully asked me if I had any 'garbage' I might have wanted to discard. This I considered a particularly thoughtful service and handed over a small polythene bag with banana skins and empty cereal bar wraps – little did I know how I was going to regret that.

On our way to Air Services' most impressive airside lounge, I had a good view of the spectacular operation that goes on relentlessly in Honolulu airport. As well as a large number of passenger flights, there is an amazing level of cargo aircraft activity ranging from the big to the enormous, enabling a large proportion of goods to quickly transit between these islands and the rest of the United States.

In the comfort of the private lounge I was visited by two efficient and polite officials from customs and immigration – this is what the ultimate VIP treatment must be about! It has to be said that the thought of how much this was going to cost me did spoil the experience a little.

Due to a shortage of nearby accommodation, Air Services eventually found me a hotel some way away from the airport. At the end of a long taxi ride, this turned out to be the Pagoda Hotel which, as the name suggests, was Chinese through and through. Their only available accommodation was an enormous and excellent apartment with twin bedrooms, a huge lounge, kitchen and bathroom – a fair sized family would find it spacious and all this for US$131/£71.

Before crashing into bed, I popped out to a twenty-four hour Cantonese restaurant just around the corner. Their food was very good, but as it was 2.00 a.m. and I was exhausted, I couldn't consume more than a small portion of the fantastic selection with which I was presented. The matriarchal cashier thought that leaving so much food untouched was the reason I was so skinny! I took that as a sideways compliment, although it occurred to me that being in the full swing of this adventure for a fortnight must have been the equivalent of participating in a very strict slimming programme.

Chapter 14
HONOLULU AND THE FLIGHT ACROSS THE ISLANDS

As Chinese as the Pagoda Hotel was, breakfast was designed for its actual location and clientele and was therefore very American. It was served in the elaborately water-themed restaurant and I found the amount of food overwhelming after what had been a fortnight of reasonably-sensible and certainly widely-spaced meals. Pleasant as they were, the waterfalls and the ponds with their fish and aquatic plants blended much too well with the weather outside. The rain hadn't stopped and there was no sign of the weather lifting, but I summoned all my available optimism and booked out of the hotel. As well as being foolhardy, I really didn't want a family apartment and, if at all possible, I would have preferred to be a lot closer to the airport.

The whole experience of this day felt somewhat strange – first of all this was the morning of Tuesday 14th and I had left Tarawa the morning of the day before, which of course was also the morning of Tuesday 14th! Then there was the whole cultural difference between Kiribati and the USA: there I had refuelled a car in a petrol station entirely made of palm trees; here a group of people I had seen the previous night repairing a road seemed to have more power tools and gadgets than the whole of Bonriki airport and certainly more lights. Amazing contrasts, how this affects the quality of life of those concerned is something at which I wouldn't like to venture a guess. Then there was the weather. Apart from the rain constantly coming down from the leaden clouds, once I got back to the splendid planning facilities of Air Services, it was obvious that this weather wasn't going to improve, let alone clear before the following day. I decided to make the best of my time in Honolulu. The efficient and friendly girls on the front desk booked me a hotel room near the airport and arranged for a hire car so I could get around Oahu, the island on which Honolulu is situated.

Before leaving the airport for the day I had to make sure the aircraft was in good order and went to the local 'service center' to sort out whatever had caused the autopilot to misbehave the previous day. There I met Steve Prankerd, the technical manager and an expatriate from Bristol who was most helpful and knowledgeable. Steve quickly diagnosed the problem as water in the static tubing, most probably due to condensation caused by the very high tropical moisture.[10] After disconnecting the tubing from the instruments, a dose of compressed Hawaiian air cleared it all.

As the airport is towards the west end of the city and Pearl Harbor is just a little further in that direction, going to see this historical location seemed a good way to spend the afternoon.

Although Pearl Harbor may well only be a short distance away, I hadn't taken into account the amazing amount of traffic on the roads. Hawaii is a beautifully isolated group of islands in the Pacific but it is also an American state and its capital, Honolulu, is a big modern city with as much traffic as any other major American city. By the time I got to Pearl Harbor the actual museum had closed and what remained accessible was not terribly interesting, but certainly a place not to be ignored due to its importance in history. Returning to Honolulu and checking in at

at the Hotel Plaza, just a stone's throw from the airport, I couldn't honestly say I was overwhelmed by the facilities. Starting with the view, all I could see from my room was an elevated part of the Nimitz highway at the same height as the window and the sight of a sodden eight-lane road with the roar of traffic hardly muffled by the double glazing was not inspiring, nor was the restaurant for that matter. The move away from my extra large Chinese apartment no longer seemed such a good idea.

Above: An urban view from my hotel room in Waikiki
Below: More rain coming to Waikiki beach
Opposite: Diamond Head from Waikiki

The following day, booking out of my 'traffic surveillance room' and booking into the Marriott Waikiki Beach Resort Hotel felt extravagant, but it did cheer me up no end – luxury therapy at its most invigorating! Despite the weather, exploring Honolulu and Waikiki was also very enjoyable, but I would not have liked to do so without a car. This city is all-American and it is not laid out in a pedestrian-friendly way. It was interesting to observe that the ethnic make-up of the population of Honolulu, apart from a strong Chinese presence, has large numbers of Japanese – curious considering the events in Pearl Harbor and the unhealed wound they inflicted on American pride.

Returning to Air Services I met Eve, the pilot of a local King Air aircraft, who helped me with the finer points of using available technology for flight information and planning. Unfortunately we found out the awful weather wasn't going anywhere. What's more, I vaguely recalled that when

I had been about to start my flight from England the weather was bad in Hawaii even then. I had simply discounted the possibility of that situation lasting long enough to constitute a problem. This was a wrong assumption and the obvious persistence of this bad weather didn't bode well for the immediate future.

Having the opportunity to indulge in the facilities of the Waikiki Beach Hotel certainly made a change from the last fortnight. The delights of western luxury ranged from washing my flight suits in the laundry, through enjoying its restaurants, to relaxing in my excellent room on the seventeenth floor with a glorious view of the city. This was especially inspiring at night when the weather actually allowed a clear view. Being able to sit on my balcony enjoying the night view after a good meal, allowed me to take stock of my situation and see how the overall picture was shaping up.

The world record for the circumnavigation had simply slipped away from me as the delay in Bonriki meant I didn't have any slack left in my timetable – and the weather in Hawaii finished it off. I can't really say I was unduly distraught by this realisation. I was well aware from the beginning that any number of different factors could have caused this and the weather was the one that I couldn't control and most likely to catch me out. And there was nothing I could do about it, I simply accepted it, despite the fact that Hawaii was the last place on earth I expected bad weather! Anyway, I had already established some world records and there were still plenty of others to chase. Of those possible I could still attempt, the most notable was the British circumnavigation record for the class. Much more importantly than all these records, the greatest possible achievement of this journey was still to get all the way around the world and become one of only sixty pilots ever to have achieved this in a single-engine aircraft.

On Thursday my daily visit to Air Services didn't find any improvement in the weather forecast and it was suggested to me that a visit to the FAA Flight Service Center might give me a better long-term picture. This visit was the most fantastic revelation! The service that American pilots receive from these places is the sort of thing we can only dream about in Europe. Here pilots have all the information they can possibly want: they can discuss trends and possibilities with specialists for as long as they need; they can take all the print-outs they might possibly want and all this is for free – including access through a free-phone number from anywhere in the country as well as the faxing of weather charts. This enlightened view clearly considers that it makes economic sense to promote safety rather than deal with the aftermath of weather-related accidents.

My visit to the flight service center gave me reason to be a little more optimistic than of late. There was a good chance of having reasonable weather to go across to Hilo the following day in order to be placed for the crossing to California once the weather allowed for that long flight. Hilo is in the eastern part of the island of Hawaii – also known as the Big Island for obvious reasons, and to distinguish it from the archipelago as a whole. Hilo is also the nearest Hawaiian airfield to the mainland, but still at a distance of 2,025nm (3,750km)! At last it looked as if I was going to start moving.

The rest of the day was spent being a tourist. I had another look around Waikiki and then drove slightly further along the coast to visit Diamond Head, an extinct volcano crater that is one of the better known touristic attractions of the island. The huge floor of the crater, with a diameter of 3,500ft (1,070m), is reached by a road tunnel through its wall and there is a footpath to the top of the 760ft (232m) high rim. Just as I got there the sun decided to make an appearance and it became incredibly hot, in fact too hot for me considering my lack of hat and water, so I decided to abandon the climb at about three quarters of the way up. Sun stroke is never welcome, particularly for a pilot.

Above: Climbing inside Diamond Head's crater
Opposite: Maui cliffs, the highest in the world

In the evening Willy Tashima, who I met through Eve the previous day at the airport, invited me for dinner at his home. Willy is a double 'Earthrounder', a retired airline captain (with more flying hours than most of us have had hot dinners) and has exceptional local knowledge. He was also a very nice person and extremely generous with his advice and practical help. At the airport he also found time to show me around his circumnavigating Bonanza, a most impressively prepared aircraft. At his beautiful home with a magnificent view of the sea, I was honoured to meet his wife Lilly, a professor at the local university. Willy once again shared with me his huge experience with marvellous specific advice. For my flight to Hilo he gave me two great pieces of information. One was how to obtain the most spectacular departure procedure from Honolulu and the other, how to avoid strong turbulence from the very high mountains of the islands between Oahu and Hawaii and still enjoy their views. Regarding the big crossing to California, he was good enough to spend a lot of time showing me how pressure patterns develop in that area and highlighting the fact that the shortest crossing, from Hilo to San Jose (next door to San Francisco), was not always the best bet. The splendid meal prepared by Lilly in their home with their friendly and stimulating conversation was a fabulous way to finish the day.

On booking out of the hotel on Friday morning, three things became obvious: the various hotels were actually not that different from each other in price; they all have taxes extra to the advertised rates; and Honolulu is not cheap.

The next round of fees came when booking out of Air Services: the total came to US$750/£405 to include $7.45 for landing; $5.00 for parking; $395.00 for handling; $95.00 for US Customs; $5.13 for taxes; $107.09 for hire car and the one that completely floored me – $111.43 for 'incineration of foreign garbage'! This was the price of having my little bag of banana skins and cereal bar wrappers thrown away. Keeping it in my pocket and dumping it later in the nearest 'trash bin' would have been a much better idea.

Starting up for my short flight of just 188nm (348km) to Hilo, I followed Willy's advice and requested an 04 highway departure. As the name suggests, this local standard departure consists of flying an extremely short distance to the overhead of the Nimitz highway and then following it

through the centre of Honolulu and to just north of Diamond Head, all at under 1,200ft. It just doesn't get more spectacular than that. The rest of my route benefited once more from my new-found Hawaiian knowledge and tracked to the north of Molokai and Maui islands, as the prevailing north-easterly wind can be funnelled between the 10,000ft high mountains of Maui and create violent turbulence to the south of the island. As the cloud base was only around 1,500ft for most of the journey, I stayed below that altitude and enjoyed the view, relaxed in the knowledge that there was plenty of time to cover what amounted to be only one eleventh of the distance of my last flight. Going past Molokai at such a low height allowed me to have a good look at the peninsula of Kalaupapa, the leper colony that became renowned world-wide in the nineteenth century.

Kalaupapa was selected for that purpose because the sheer mountain cliffs right against its base created a natural barrier that ensured segregation from the rest of the island, as was common practice in those days. It was here that the work of Father Damien became famous by giving back human dignity to those people suffering from such a feared condition. Thankfully times are now different, but it is obvious how these people were isolated from the rest of the world as the cliffs of the north coast of Molokai are supposed to be the highest in the world. As I flew just off the coast, the sheer black mountain sides disappeared upwards into the cloud at around 1,800ft and because of the previous rain they were spectacularly cut by numerous monumental waterfalls – a fantastic sight.

Approaching the Big Island, the cloud base lowered somewhat to around 1,000ft, making sure the two volcanoes were totally hidden from view. A good part of the circuit of runway 03 of Hilo International Airport was carried out above the town offering me a splendid view of ex-otic trees, colonial style houses and an interesting seafront. Once on the ground I couldn't have wished for a more enthusiastic and friendly reception at the Hilo branch of Air Services, as Terri Thomas and Tim Lewis helped me find a sheltered spot to tie down the aircraft and arranged, with some difficulty, a hotel room. Being parked next to a couple of dilapidated agricultural aircraft made me idly wonder if they were in that state because they had been waiting for flyable weather for the last five years!

Chapter 15
HILO TO SAN JOSE

Air Services had booked a room for me at the Hilo Hawaiian, supposedly the best hotel in town and seemingly the only one with vacancies for the day of my arrival, Friday 17th March. Arriving at this hotel was not unlike discovering a comedy set – in fact I thought I had found the real Fawlty Towers all these miles away.

The receptionist had the most amazing beehive hairdo I had ever seen (even in the sixties), and she had probably exhausted her sense of humour creating it, as there wasn't any left for the job. After establishing that they didn't have any more rooms for the actual weekend, she went on to make quite clear that there was no way she could possibly notify me of any possible cancellations. With that a room key was slid across the counter in my direction (as it wasn't actually thrown at my head, I assumed she must have liked me) and I was dispatched to the sixth floor.

As I was unlocking the door of the room, I had a strange feeling that there was somebody already there – and there was! As I cautiously opened the door, a sleepy woman rose from a bed prompting apologies, embarrassment and a phone call to reception. 'Big Hair' wouldn't offer any apologies and the only solution available was for me to go back to reception and collect another key. Once again back on the sixth floor and four doors away from the rudely-awakened lady, I could have been forgiven for thinking that the situation was improving as I didn't find another sleepy woman – in fact I didn't find anything at all as the key wouldn't open the door! So it was back down to reception for yet another key and again no word of apology. I understood that the advice issued with the second key consisted of words to the effect that they weren't going to entertain demands of guests actually wanting to occupy their rooms, so if the second key was going to fail to work, I was to wait in the corridor for a maintenance man sent up to check the lock. This time the key actually worked, there were no women in bed and the maintenance man turned up about half an hour later – a marvellous start.

Despite the weather having offered me a window to reposition to Hilo, there was no immediate opportunity to go across to California, so I was hoping to be able to discover more of the Big Island in-between checking meteorological forecasts and route calculations, to say nothing about the need to find a room for the weekend.

The Hilo Hawaiian, like most hotels in Hilo, was on Banyan Drive – named after the many such spectacular trees all along it. These were the trees I had noticed just before I landed and I went on to discover that many had been planted by celebrities throughout the twentieth century, from politicians such as Richard Nixon to film stars, religious leaders and adventurers such as Amelia Earhart. Just as with most of the town of Hilo, some of these trees had been destroyed by tsunamis and several have been replanted. The two most notable features of these trees, as well as being held as holy in some parts of the world, are their aerial roots (which can extend from the branches right to the ground) and the ability of the whole plant to be able to expand to several acres, providing a splendid shelter from the elements. I certainly greatly enjoyed an evening walk under their shade.

One of the great views from Hilo and specifically from this hotel was the sight of Mauna Kea volcano, which simply means White Mountain because its summit is covered in deep snow. However, apart from in the early morning, this view is seldom available as clouds rapidly form throughout the day and completely obscure the top of this dormant volcano. An interesting and much quoted statistic in Hawaii about this 13,796ft (4,205m) high volcano is that it is 32,000ft (9,754m) above the sea bed, making it the tallest mountain on earth, Mount Everest included.

Enjoying these aspects of nature was going to be greatly spoilt if I didn't have a room in which to sleep and after making a few enquiries around nearby hotels I was starting to think that I may have to sleep in the aircraft. Roughing it up in Hawaii wasn't appealing. A call to the emergency phone of Air Services meant Tim came to the rescue and found a hotel for me, only some 300 metres from my original one. This place had the grand name of Country Club Hawaii, and although there was nothing actually wrong with it, both the clientele and the general feel of the place gave an impression of an abode for displaced people. I thought of it, unfairly, as my 'refugee camp' – but I didn't forget that any room is better than no room. One of the more unusual aspects of this hotel was the fact that the 'lobby' was outside. This lobby was supposed to have internet wireless access, which I never found a way to use, and a couple of computers with several keyboard keys not operational presumably due to the high humidity of a very wet Hilo.

Of the few restaurants I tried, Uncle Billy's advertised itself as having free Hula shows in the evening, so I was looking forward to discovering first hand Polynesian music and dances. The food was simple and good in an American way, the entertainment was not quite what I had anticipated and I thought the dances were particularly well suited for performers with a solid frame. It was of course a free show, so I didn't have any complaints. Well, maybe just the one about never seeing a grass skirt in all of my time in Hawaii – after all the posters showing the delights of these islands, this has to stand as a major misrepresentation!

Top: Banyan Drive
Above: The snow-capped Mauna Kea volcano above the palm trees

In between rain showers on Sunday, I walked to Air Services to have a look around and check the aeroplane. There I found Terri on duty which was quite for-tunate as she appeared to be permanently cheerful and always full of optimism. After showing me around the airport, Terri arranged a hire car which was a great way to escape my hotel room. What was not quite so great was the weather – amazingly, Hilo is the town with the greatest an-nual rainfall in the world, so much so that rain is the subject of quite a lot of local jokes. On top of this and throughout the time I was there, the weather was exceptionally bad all over the Hawaiian Islands and that amounted to an awful lot of bad weather!

The intensity of the rain was something I hadn't experienced since my time in equatorial Africa in the sixties, during my Portuguese military service. The Hawaiian rain was the cause of two reservoirs on different islands bursting their dams with some loss of life, as well as the crash of a fixed-wing ambulance with the loss of the crew. From a more personal and trivial viewpoint, the weather was sufficiently bad for a number of roads to be made impassable with floods and mud slides, so my new-found freedom with a hire car was severely curtailed . The most notable omission to my sight-seeing was the monument to Captain James Cook, built on the spot where he was killed in February 1779 on the west coast of the island.

From my numerous phone calls to the flight information center (FIC) of Honolulu, it started to look as if there might be some good local weather on Monday and a reasonable chance of being able to go across to California the night of Tuesday to Wednesday.

Monday was indeed a beautiful day and I decided to take advantage of that weather by going flying to the active volcano. The flight south was the only chance I had to travel any distance away from Hilo and it was most enjoyable to see the Big Island from low altitude. Getting near the south coast I came across quite a lot of cloud and only when I got to the actual coast did I realise that I was flying over molten lava – not a great place to have an engine failure and I wondered if the result would have been aviator *en croûte*, or *pilot flambé*. The sight of this lava entering the sea and the resultant column of steam rising was one of the most impressive natural sights I have ever had the good fortune to witness. There was no doubt that this steam was at

Opposite: The active crater of Kilauea
Above: The hot lava entering the sea

least partially responsible for the clouds over the coast, the very same clouds I had to go under to have a look at the actual active volcano crater. At first glance this crater, Kilauea (Much Spreading), appears to be an outlet on the side of its larger neighbour, Mauna Loa (Long Mountain), but in reality it has been shown to be geologically quite separate.

Kilauea is not a dramatic conical volcano as its lava is much too fluid for that (hence the name) but at the time it was the biggest active volcano on earth. Taking photographs of the crater was not an easy operation as there were a number of helicopters taking tourists on sight-seeing trips and despite maintaining the correct direction of traffic around there, I couldn't match their low speed and it was a hectic time. While on the overhead of the crater, I made sure to stick to the advice I was given about not flying through any volcano smoke as apparently that sort of incursion causes an engine stoppage.

Returning to the airport, I found the view of Banyan Drive more interesting than ever as by then I knew it from the ground and could identify some of its trees and lawns.

Tuesday 21st March (local) was spent calculating the route to Santa Barbara in California, rechecking the aircraft, arranging the refuelling, filing the flight plan and trying to rest. Before trying to get some sleep in the evening, I rang the FIC once more to make sure everything was still favouring the flight plan to Santa Barbara. As always they couldn't have been more helpful and after a full hour of detailed discussion regarding the possible position of a slight high pressure centre squeezed by the two major low pressure systems between Hawaii and California, I decided to go to San Jose instead. So it was a matter of recalculating everything, re-filing the flight plan on the phone and by the time all was sorted out it was time to go – so much for an invigorating sleep!

Once back at Air Services, Terri had to call for an official from the US Department of Agriculture (USDA) as it is a legal requirement that all flights from Hawaii to the mainland are checked to ensure no prohibited fruits or vegetables are taken there. Terri, who took it on herself to look after me during my extended stay in Hilo, maintaining she was doing that because of her maternal instincts (despite the relative ages pointing in the opposite direction), had arranged for a ferry-flight discounted handling fee of only US$195/£105, pretty much a 50% discount.

The rain had managed to hold off until I was ready to close the canopy. As I started the engine in the increasing rain and started taxiing away, the sight of Terri on her own waving me away in a wet and deserted airport gave the occasion a special feel. So, after eight days on the islands of Hawaii, the long flight to the mainland was going to start, just as the control tower was closing for the night.

In a strange sort of way, lining up on Hilo's runway 08 with over 2,000nm (3,800km) of Pacific to go before the Californian coast didn't feel quite as intimidating as the departure from Bonriki. Undoubtedly the presence of runway lights and an efficient and informative control tower helped a lot, despite the poor weather.

But the resultant relaxation was soon to change, the first few minutes of the flight made sure of that. First of all, on the initial climb out, I suffered from the worst case of the 'leans' I have ever experienced. This condition is caused by the brain being tricked into thinking that the body is leaning when in fact it isn't, or vice-versa, hence the name. Sometimes the brain whispers that message quietly, sometimes louder – in this case it was shouting and it took all my training and willpower to believe the aircraft's instruments and not my sense of balance. I think the cause of this upset was being able to see lights, both my own and those on the ground, on my left side and nothing at all on my right side, not to mention seeing no horizon line at all. The combination of these factors led me to be absolutely convinced that the aircraft was flying level when in fact it was progressively turning to the left. This is a recognisable phenomenon for pilots without available visual references. The brain can and is easily fooled by conditions when the information received from the various senses is contradictory. This is particularly confusing when in an aeroplane and one cannot even be sure of what is up or down![11] All this brings us to a golden rule of long life in aviation – if you do not have some sort of instrument rating and suitable instrumentation, don't even think of flying without visual references.

Possibly because of this unsettling episode I forgot to retract the flaps on time and was lucky not to have caused serious damage to them by flying at a speed higher than permissible for extended flaps. All in all, not a great start.

The next problem occurred when trying to transfer from VHF to HF. The HF set wasn't functioning as expected. This was partially caused by the HF radio being well over the far side of the panel and the control buttons both small and close together. It was quite a while before I discovered I had pressed two buttons at the same time and entered a function from which I was slow to identify and exit.

Once HF communications were established satisfactorily it was then time to settle down to a very dark crossing, as the moon wouldn't be rising until very late. Entertainment was provided by the sight of the navigation lights of airliners well above me and following the same route. Being able to match the navigation lights of aircraft with their position calls on the radio provided more fun than it was reasonable to expect.

The traffic in this airway was busier than I had expected into the small hours when it finally tailed off. The only irritating distraction was the failure of the bulb illuminating the altimeter, a situation which I partially solved by replacing it with the bulb from the vertical speed indicator.

The weather was not much different from the accurate forecast I had received in Hilo, reasonably uneventful with the exception of some large cumulus that created the now-familiar static electricity sparking to the top of the instrument glare shield along with some turbulence and a steady light headwind.

Just as forecast, the outside air temperature (OAT) was slowly dropping all the time towards the mainland and the new day brought the sight of a lot of cloud below me with the tops at an estimated 5-6,000ft and bases at around 2,000ft. As the day progressed the gaps got smaller and smaller while the tops got higher and higher until they were at well over 10,000ft, changing the view from rather pleasant to miserable and cold. Ice began to form on the leading edges of the wings and all over the windscreen, at first quite fast, then appearing to stabilise with an estimated half inch (13mm) thickness.

This was bad news! Ice can turn wings into planks, and as planks don't fly well it was time to be concerned. The fact that the nearest land was around 1,000nm (1,850km) away also helped to concentrate the mind. Descending was, of course, the obvious answer, but the higher headwinds at lower levels and the aforementioned distance to land didn't make that possibility particularly attractive. While weighing my options, I had plenty to keep watch over. The wings were only visible if I pushed myself backwards to see behind the ice covering the canopy, but there was no apparent further increase on the wings and the tailplane was relatively free of ice. The air intake to the carburettor was held permanently on the 'hot' position to avoid ice formation on the air filter and the subsequent engine stoppage. Just as I started to get concerned about the HF aerial that had grown to around one inch (25mm) thick with ice, the engine lost power and I felt a lot of vibration from the forward end. This was the stuff of nightmares!

But this was reality and I was on my way to the only available course of action – descending below the freezing level as expeditiously as possible without risking overspeeding for the conditions and maintaining an even closer look on the ice build-up. Sometime during that descent the HF aerial started to whip around furiously and no amount of speed variation seemed to improve it.[12] The possibility of the aerial breaking was almost too awful to contemplate; being so far away from land with no engine power and unable to communicate with anybody was unthinkable.

Fortunately the aerial survived and so did I – below 5,000ft the ice began coming off the wings and aerial leaving only the canopy iced up. Thankfully the engine also resumed power without undue vibrations, presumably because the air filter and the propeller were freed of their ice. The ice covering of the canopy stayed there for quite some time, surprisingly moving around by freely floating on the canopy itself until it blew off in one go, mercifully without damage to the tail surfaces.

The flight was then able to continue at under 5,000ft without any possibility of regaining my previous level as the temperature never recovered and I certainly had had enough of icing over oceans to last me a lifetime.

San Francisco radio was again a comforting voice with their excellent service and, by going outside standard radio service on a few occasions, gave a human touch to the otherwise impersonal data exchange. They asked about my wellbeing on behalf of Air Services Hawaii and checked if I agreed with having a TV crew waiting for me upon my arrival in San Jose. Being told that the quality of my HF transmissions were better than most light aircraft in that crossing was also a boost, especially in view of my modest equipment.

The winds did change from a headwind into a tailwind just as forecast and so the speed for the journey was good, in fact faster than planned.

When it eventually appeared, the distant sight of the Californian coast, just discernible through the mist, went straight to the top of my list of the most beautiful views ever. This became even more special as I recognised the opening of San Francisco bay from a long way away and above all I was looking at solid ground after what had been a difficult, long and tiring crossing.

I found the approach into San Jose absolutely fabulous. First of all the view was glorious with the back-drop of the Sierra tops covered in snow and the welcoming state of California offering a visual diversity much appreciated after hours and hours of Pacific. The very high density of air traffic of all types going about their business in a splendidly co-ordinated fashion was fascinating to me, what a fantastic example of an efficient system. The actual airport, with its three parallel runways, is right in the middle of a huge urban sprawl and is mainly used by business jets. The top of the tallest building seemed to be in line with the ILS for the centre runway. This was clearly not the case in reality, but after fifteen hours of flying over the Pacific, it looked close to me.

The arrival in San Jose certainly was a memorable event. After landing and being directed to the San Jose Jet Center (SJC, my handling company), I couldn't have wished for a better reception, starting with the SJC hostesses rolling out a red carpet (literally) to G-RV. The enthusiasm of all present, from the man with the chocks to the CEO filled me with delight and surprise. Not only was everyone uninhibited in their praise and help, but they were also considerate enough to make sure I had time to think if I needed some rest before the TV crew were allowed to approach me.

I elected to go ahead with the interviews straight away. I was so tired that a rest would simply have sent me off to sleep without hope of waking up sufficiently to have a sensible conversation. Despite having been in the air for fifteen hours and twenty-eight minutes, I was glad I did. The professionalism of the reporter was evident in all aspects of the interview, from the obviously well-researched background to being able to capture the essence of the whole adventure with accurate and succinct wording, without resorting to sentimentalism.

Booking into SJC without the need for customs (this was just a flight from one American state to another!) revealed an amazingly plush facility with an exemplary professional service. G-RV was also beautifully taken care of and placed in the most splendid hangar. Finally SJC booked me into one of the best hotels in San Jose and provided a driver to take me there.

The Hotel De Anza was very impressive with its marbled and expensive furnishings, but the room was very small and I had to call reception to get all manner of things that should have been there and weren't, giving the staff occasion to show how poor the service was. As eating was a priority and I had to struggle to stay awake, I went for a brisk walk around the block to find a restaurant I fancied. As that was unsuccessful, I went back to the hotel and tried one of its own restaurants. This was a pleasant surprise as their Italian restaurant offered excellent food, good service at a very reasonable price. Shame I was too tired to fully appreciate it. Once back in my room I was in a deep sleep before my head touched the pillow.

In the morning, after being collected from the hotel by a courtesy car from SJC, I found G-RV already outside the hangar basking in the beautifully bright and warm Californian morning in the company of a local Vans RV-4. SJC continued the VIP treatment with polished professionalism and after refuelling the aircraft at a much discounted rate, provided me with a deliciously extravagant pastry-based breakfast to take in my flight to Abilene in Texas, my next planned stop.

Taxiing out to depart on the shorter runway, I couldn't help myself marvelling at the glorious weather and in a 'country-boy-coming-to-the-big-city' kind of way, the splendid facilities of San Jose airport.

What followed was undeniably exciting for all the wrong reasons. On the take-off run, just after raising the tailwheel, I felt one hiccup from the engine which I decided to ignore as it continued to develop full power – bad decision! Very soon after the main wheels left the ground the engine started to seriously misfire. The memory of the airport surrounded by city flashed through my mind, reminding me that San Jose was not a good place to have an engine failure – the only reasonable thing to do was to land on what was left of the runway ahead of me. A combination of high speed, short available runway and excess weight made the next few seconds quite busy and as the barriers at the end were looming large, I actually considered provoking a ground loop to stop before hitting them.[13] Fortunately this was not necessary and I came to a halt with an uncomfortably small margin, but without any damage, other than very hot and smoking brakes.

After exiting the runway, I carried out many engine run-ups without reaching any conclusion and I simply had to abandon the departure and head back to the maintenance facility for a closer inspection.

Chapter 16
SAN JOSE TO ABILENE

The staff of the local maintenance shop, Corporate Air Technology, were both prompt and thorough in investigating the mysterious misfire. As most engineers are devoid of hangerside manners, they fired questions at me immediately, like what the values of exhaust gas temperatures (EGT) were when the misfire occurred – as if I had time to look at that! Or that such a thought had even crossed my mind…

However the big problem was that despite our joint efforts we never found a fault of any sorts. So after a few hours of careful and systematic searching we had to come to the conclusion that there was simply nothing to be found. This, of course, meant that I would have to take off again without knowing what had been or might still be wrong with the engine, not a situation I was happy with. In fact, once I took into consideration the size of the city around the airport it made me increasingly nervous.

I was further frustrated as by then it was much too late to go direct to Abilene in Texas, my next scheduled stopover. After a look at the relevant charts, I decided to try to follow my original track and land just before nightfall. Apple Valley on the edge of the desert, north-east of Los Angeles became my target for the day – but even that was assuming I was going to take off without any more problems.

Taxiing out certainly wasn't carried out as lightly as in the previous occasion. My plan was to climb on the overhead of the airfield to a comfortable height and if everything was running well I would then set course as planned. Unsurprisingly, the pre-flight checks were carried out in the most pedantic way, which I can excel at!

When it came to check the hot air intake for the carburettor it all became clear: despite having been a warm (around 23°C), cloudless morning my previous problem was just due to ice in the carburettor, as simple as that. My previous hurried flick through that part of the pre-flight check didn't spot it, after all, how silly can it be to think of ice in such

Carburettor icing can stop an engine and usually occurs at ambient temperatures significantly above 0°C, surprisingly much more likely than at temperatures significantly below this point. This is often due to the temperature inside the venturi of the carburettor being lowered by the drop in air pressure and the cooling effect of the evaporating fuel. As ice can only occur when water is present, the proximity of the dew point to the ambient temperature is an excellent indicator of this danger. The possibility of heating the incoming air is the usual answer to this problem, despite other negative consequences of such a solution.

a beautiful Californian morning? Admittedly, if I had allowed myself to take in that the automated terminal information service (ATIS) was giving the dew point at just below ambient temperature, it would have been obvious that these were the perfect conditions for carburettor icing to form. I had clearly been suffering from selective hearing...

By the time I took off the second time everything went perfectly and it was a slightly wiser pilot that set course to Apple Valley.

The views flying down the San Joaquin Valley were an absolute delight. The snow-capped Sierra Nevada along with the multiple agricultural activities and the villages in the valley all amounted to a splendid diversity that the many previous hours over the sea just couldn't offer.

Crossing the lower reaches of the Sierra, the presence of the largest wind farm I have ever seen came as quite a surprise. I simply wasn't aware of such an interest in renewable energy existing in the USA. On the other hand, I was well aware of their obsession with security and, when in contact with Mojave airport, I wasn't really surprised when ATC showed great concern about the "origin of the aircraft", no doubt prompted by its unfamiliar registration format.[14] Stating that "Golf, Golf, Delta, Romeo, Victor (G-GDRV) is a British aircraft" in what sounded to me the most pompous tone I could muster, suitably reassured the controller and she appeared much calmer from then on.

Mojave airport itself, as well as the nearby Edwards Air Base, were highlights of this journey

with their historical importance intrinsically linked with their role at the cutting edge of aviation and space travel. Just thinking that I was flying over the home base of Burt Rutan, one of the world's most innovative and prolific aircraft designers actually blurring the line between air and space travel, and the airfield from where most of those aircraft took to the air (and I am sure are still taking place) was a most exciting experience.[15] Admiring the huge Edwards AB runway where the space shuttle has so often landed was also rather special.

The Mojave desert itself offered a great performance of light effects, aided by the low evening sun exaggerating the shapes of rock formations with an astonishing contrast between various tones of red

A spectacular pass in the Mojave desert

and the stark black of the shadows. This resulted in a masterpiece of natural art that simply couldn't be viewed without emotion from my glorious best-seat-in-the-house position.

To balance this ecstasy, the security restrictions around the many military zones in this area made sure that I stayed firmly connected with the real world. It was quite clear that they were not going to allow any foreign aeroplanes to stray into their military airspace.

Apple Valley is built on a plateau of over 3,000ft altitude with mountains both to the east and west of around 6,000ft, creating a density altitude with which I wasn't familiar and it nearly caught me out as I was also still carrying a great deal of fuel. The combination of thin air and great weight brought the stall warning buzzer screaming well before I had expected it. A combination of a prompt lowering of the nose and a handful of power averted disaster and although I used much of the 4,000ft (1,220m) runway, I still managed to land without having to go around. It just goes to show that it's not over until it's over…

And it's not over until it's parked and secured! As there was no manned tower I had to find my own way around the almost deserted airfield and went to park next to a solitary Grumman AA-5 being tied down by its pilot. While also tying down G-RV to the provided permanent loops in the parking positions and thinking that the wind must at times really blow through the airfield, a pick-up truck came over driven by the local engineer. ATC had rang to ask him to see that everything was OK with my flight as I hadn't closed my flight plan. Oops! Unlike Britain, most countries require flight plans to be actively closed and I had forgotten but the chap in the pick-up was kind enough to offer to close my flight plan for me. For this I was most thankful, and felt suitably chastised. I did feel that this system is better than ours, where a search and rescue operation is only initiated if there is an actual notification of a flight not arriving. Maybe this can make the difference between surviving and not, if it all goes wrong.

The pilot of the aircraft next to me was one Bob Thompson and he was most helpful with local advice and a lift to Victorville some ten miles away where he delivered me to a good and reasonably-priced hotel, offering to collect me again in the morning.

After a pleasant meal and my usual telephone chat with Jill, I made a phone call to Abilene to update them with my progress as it was from that Texan town that the local EAA Chapter had so enthusiastically asked me to stop over there. Unfortunately I forgot the time difference between California and Texas and went on to wake people up in the middle of the night – not such a great way to impress my hosts for the following day. Unlike them, nobody woke me up and I had a good night's sleep until 5.00 a.m. local. As always, my first thoughts of the day were concerned with the weather ahead, so my first priority was to telephone the FIC.

Talking to them, I learnt about a meteorological phenomenon I didn't even know could possibly exist: cold fronts without clouds! When I asked the forecaster how a cold front could possibly be conciliated with expected clear skies, the answer was both surprising and simple: the moisture of the cold front precipitates over the mountain ranges inland from the coast, so by the time it arrives over the desert there's no moisture left, only the different air masses and the associated wind changes. I suppose this also helps to explain why the desert is there in the first place…

Admittedly, this wasn't my first meteorological lesson in this part of the world. When I returned to my room the previous night and upon washing my underclothes, I was amazed to see them dried literally within minutes of hanging them in the bathroom. To start with I had put this down to good ventilation, but the truth became eventually obvious – there is no moisture in the desert.

After the huge all-American breakfast that makes any non-American forget about food for the rest of the day, Bob and his wife came over to take me to the airfield again, demonstrating the help and enthusiasm I experienced from flyers all over the USA. However, once airborne and in my haste to wave at them by rocking the wings very low over the runway, I almost scared myself as the tip tanks were still full and it nearly got out of hand – I didn't do that again!

Leaving Apple Valley I had occasion to sample how well the Unicom radio frequency works. With no manned tower, everybody (and there was quite a lot of commuter air traffic at that time of the morning) transmits their positions and intentions over the published frequency so we all know what each other is doing, and it all works beautifully.

Above: The Colorado river
Below: Mountains with El Paso in the distance

My route to Abilene first followed a south-easterly track to Tucson. The views over the desert were just as breathtaking as on the previous day, always dazzling with ever-changing sculptured hills and glorious colours and stark shadows. Add to this the snaking roads through spectacular passes, the Colorado river and Tucson with its mountain backdrop and it all amounted to a magnificent visual feast. The downside of being so taken by this natural spectacle was that I managed to miss one of the greatest sights to any aviation enthusiast. I completely missed the famous aircraft graveyard near Tucson where thousands of disused air force aircraft of all types are put to rest. Much later on looking at one of my

photographs, I could actually see a corner of it right under my track. But at the time I never saw it – such is life!

After Tucson my heading became more easterly and after touching El Paso right on the Mexican border, I crossed the salt flats towards the lower reaches of the Rocky Mountains.

It was along this part of New Mexico where I fully appreciated how fast opposing traffic can grow, from a speck in the windscreen to a full-size aeroplane in such a short space of time, too short to take any action. At the time, as throughout the United States, I was recieving a most efficient radar information service

Above: Checking position by El Paso
Below: Taxiing in Abilene *(Photograph by Dr. John Gullett)*

and I was advised of the presence of a twin-engined aircraft in the reciprocal heading only 500ft above my level, just as he was advised of my presence. As the separating distance became less and less I was surprised that I couldn't see him and obviously he couldn't see me either as we both had been asked to report the other one on sight. Just as I picked him up as a tiny dot he announced seeing me. The time it took that tiny dot, which remained the same size for quite a long time, to turn into an aircraft crossing with me at a very short distance felt like only two seconds! The closing speed must have been in the order of 300kts to 340kts.

The visibility was quite good, his aircraft was a very conspicuous bright yellow and we knew of each other's presence. Without one or more of these conditions, would we have seen each other before actually crossing? A sobering thought.

Texas made itself known in two different ways. First of all there was the sight of an incredible number of identical man-made structures extending as far as the eye could see, even from 10,000ft. It was a while before I worked out that these structures were in fact oil field pumps, commonly known as nodding donkeys. The other apparent change was the beginning of a vegetation cover, not very green, but vegetation none the less.

With less than an hour to go to Abilene, I once again experienced the relaxed and efficient ATC service found in the USA. This time it came about as I made a wide curve to miss the busy airspace of Midland airport, as in the UK such a manoeuvre often saves time and difficulty for light-aircraft traffic. However here it prompted ATC to enquire if I was lost. Controlled airspace is there to facilitate the passage of all traffic and the function of ATC is to ensure that there is separation and optimum use of their zone for all users. I can think of places in England that could learn a thing or two from them.

On the base leg to Abilene, the control tower passed a request from the local EAA Chapter asking if I would do a low pass for the media. Although it was bumpy below 6,000ft, a low and fast pass is never an opportunity to be missed. After a suitably steep pull up and tight circuit I taxied in to meet a large group of people and media welcoming me into Texas. Life was good.

Sam Evans was the first of many to introduce himself and was kind enough

not to mention my late-night call. From then on everything I wished ran smoothly, such as when I remembered that the flight plan hadn't been closed, Charlotte from ATC was already there closing it for me on her mobile. I knew I was going to enjoy my stay in Texas.

Chapter 17
A WARM WELCOME IN ABILENE

The apron around G-RV seemed to be full of people in a party mood and their genuine interest in what I was doing made me feel extremely honoured. After the TV interviews and lots of chat with enthusiastic well-wishers waving cameras, I taxied to the hangar where the aircraft was to be housed and undergo its maintenance. This huge hangar belonged to Pride Refining Inc and had to be the best-equipped private hangar I had ever seen. Although the Lear Jet was out at the time, the 'shopping' Cirrus SR22 was still there, along with a huge power boat, assorted interesting vehicles and all sorts of useful machinery. Texas has a reputation for doing things on a large scale and the Pride hangar was a good example of the Texan dimension. This was also where Lew Jones, the company's chief pilot, had his office and reigned supreme. Lew was one of the great characters I had the good fortune to meet along this journey and with his magnificent Stetson and equally glorious southern drawl, there could be no doubts at all about where he came from.

After putting G-RV to bed, Sam drove me to a restaurant with very Texan staff and typical everything else. This was where the local EAA Chapter (Chapter 471) were kind enough to host a meal to celebrate my passage through Abilene, and their hospi-

Top: In Abilene with EAA Chapter 471. L to R Gray Bridwell, Charlotte Rhodes, Sam Evans, author
Above: The author with John Gullett and Gray Bridwell in Abilene
Opposite: The cockpit in Abilene *(photograph by John Gullett)*

tality and enthusiasm was inspirational. I was left with the impression that the pioneering spirit was still very much alive over there, a situation I feel no longer exists in Europe. Some of these guys were building a variety of RV aircraft and, of course, the conversation tended not to stray away from that subject for too long, but long enough to be able to talk a little about the life of the dozen or so members present and their corner of Texas.

Regarding the food on offer, I was amazed by the steak I had, something that simply cannot be forgotten. As well as being typically Texan in size (not simply American), it must also rate as the tastiest I ever had – complete with 'cowboy sauce' strong enough to blow anyone's Stetson off their heads, except a real Texan, of course!

After the splendid meal and pleasant socialising, I was driven by Sam Evans and his wife to the comfortable motel they had booked for me. It was then that the first sign of my adventure approaching an end appeared. This took the form of a parcel Sam handed me, containing the immersion suit that I would be using for the Atlantic crossing. Jill had arranged to send the suit to Texas so I wouldn't have to carry it as dead weight for three-quarters of the way around the world. The last ocean crossing was in sight.

The combination of being relaxed by the relatively short journey of the day (a mere 884nm (1,637km), taking six hours and twenty-seven minutes and an excellent meal in great company allowed me one of the best night's sleep of the whole journey.

In the morning, following a huge breakfast, I was collected by Lew in his enormous 4x4 pick-up (difficult to imagine him driving any lesser vehicle) and he handed me a copy of the local newspaper with my picture on the front page.

Once back at the hangar and with the huge powered-doors quietly sliding open by remote control (what else?!) it was time to warm up the engine and start carrying out the planned maintenance with everything my hosts had thoughtfully and generously collected for me. Unfortunately I was not so thoughtful and only spotted I had the wrong oil once most of it was in the engine. Happily, the always resourceful Lew had a look around and soon produced the correct type and quantity of oil – two consecutive oil changes made sure that the inside of the engine was spotlessly clean.

While the engine was draining for the second time I was invited to the Chapter's barbecue on the opposite end of the airfield, the actual location was their big hangar project. They were justifiably proud of this work and I was shown around the large hangar they had leased from the airport for their exclusive use. As the building had been in a pretty poor state of repair, they had obtained the lease with a ridiculously low rent and were completely refurbishing it, including a complete new roof, at their expense. This sense of working for the good of the community, as well as being prepared to invest their own money into what amounts to a co-operative project, was something I found most commendable. The combination of individual and communal generosity had a great feel-good factor and I am sure it was conducive to many other good things.

A great place to be in great company – and they could also put together a tasty barbecue!

Once the work on the RV was finished, including 'borrowing' parts off the RV kit that Sam was building, the aircraft was re-fuelled ready for an early start the next morning. The only snag was that I came close to losing my spare flying suit when it was washed in the hangar facilities in what turned out to be the hottest cycle known to man. I think this was possibly due to Texans not limiting themselves to anything less than full power! At the same time all my attempts to pay for all the materials I had used, including the two lots of oil, the fuel itself and a few spares were simply not accepted – they just wouldn't listen to my offers of payment. Their generosity was indeed extraordinary.

One thing, or rather the only thing that Lew's office didn't have was a broadband internet connection and studying the weather for the next couple of legs took a little longer than usual, not least because everybody wanted to help with their advice. However, the problem with my planning was caused by the poor weather around the Great Lakes, with lots of snow, and the even worse situation in Newfoundland with very low cloud bases and freezing rain. There was also a cold front descending from the Oregon direction towards Texas and this wasn't going to allow me to stay put any longer to wait for the situation in the north-east to improve. In the end I thought the most sensible arrangement, subject to consultation with the FIC, was to continue due east to the coast in Georgia and then track north along the coast to Maine, therefore skirting the bad weather by a substantial margin. This however would have the effect of making the distance much further to the north-east corner of North America and would also result in a longer Atlantic crossing.

Because of this change of route I had to tell the people who were enthusiastically expecting me in Ohio that I wouldn't be able to make it there. I very much felt that when people were so supportive about what I was doing, I had a moral obligation to stick to the original plan and make an appearance. By being forced to change my plans at the last minute and not turn up I felt I was letting them down, but there just wasn't anything I could do about it.

The following day was Sunday the 26th and a lot of the clientele in the motel breakfast room arrived in their Sunday best and, in doing so, I was treated to a veritable cowboy fashion parade. This surpassed any images I might have had of the archetypal Texan cowboy and his best finery. They were all male of an age varying between 'late middle to very pensionable' wearing outrageous Stetsons, jeans ironed razor sharp and splendid cowboy boots – they were an amazing sight and I must say I really fancied those boots!

Once I had my talk with the FIC confirming that my planned route via Georgia was indeed the most sensible course of action, I went to reception to check out of the motel. Again their generosity came to surprise me as the guys from the EAA Chapter had covered all my expenses at the motel and there wasn't anything left for me to pay.

Once Lew collected and drove me to the airfield, filing the flight plan to go to Savannah in Georgia prompted great consternation regarding the remote possibility of my infringement of the prohibited airspace near Waco, south of Dallas. As I couldn't quite appreciate why it had caused such a stir, I was told that the reason for the existence of this prohibited airspace was to protect the ranch of George W Bush, a fact that had passed me by. It strikes me as odd that by placing a prohibition around a secret or sensitive area it simply highlights that location, but it happens everywhere.

It wasn't long before the rest of the 'gang' started to appear, all bearing gifts of food and drink for the journey. This gave me a bit of a problem as Charlotte Rhodes, the Chapter's female ATC officer and fantastic all-round motivator, had already showered me with food gifts by taking me shopping the previous evening and I simply didn't have anywhere to put all those delicious gifts. I just hope I didn't offend anyone with my refusals.

Chapter 18
ABILENE TO BANGOR

The splendid hangar facilities in Abilene were the ideal place in which to carry out the external pre-flight checks and spend some time loading the planned routes towards the northeast of the USA into the GPS units. Although I was actually going directly to Savannah, I really only saw this as an overnight stop and weather diversion en-route to Bangor in Maine.

A little before 8.00 a.m., Texan technology got to work and the hangar doors hummed open to an already blustery day ahead of the approaching cold front. As the aircraft was pushed outside, the wind had already reached 25kt with gusts of 30kt and was increasing, which in view of the absence of a parking brake, was enough to demand holding the aircraft on the toe brakes while carrying out my internal pre-start checks. I didn't fancy imitating the tumbleweeds cartwheeling through the airfield.

With due consideration to the crosswind strength, I taxied out to the

Top: Checking routes
Above: Pushing G-GDRV into the strong morning wind

active runway which was perfectly aligned with the wind, giving me the ideal conditions for a singularly short take-off run, despite the weight of the fuel I was carrying. Leaving the Texan soil I felt a little sadness at being parted so soon from my new-found friends.

My journey to the east benefited from continuously-changing scenery with the scrubland of western Texas gradually giving way to more substantial vegetation and the oil fields replaced by huge ranches, presumably for cattle, although I couldn't be too sure from my cruising height of 10,000ft.

Dallas soon came and went, its silhouette being very distinct to anyone that ever watched an episode of the renowned 'soap' of the same name. Although to me it appeared surprising small. I had to wonder if the word 'small' ever gets used by Texans to describe anything native and I eventually decided it wasn't very likely. While Dallas passed by on the port side, Waco and George W. Bush's ranch stayed comfortably to the south of my track keeping me well away from possible or simply imagined twitchy trigger fingers.

Further east the vegetation started to become positively lush and by the time I got to the Red river and the state of Louisiana the terrain had an appearance of great fertility. Both the Red and the Mississippi rivers were a good match to my preconceived image by being spectacularly wide with lazy bends and brown muddy waters. A steamer sailing majestically upstream the Mississippi was the prompt I needed to set my thoughts towards the social upheavals that this part of the world has known. This was, as Paul Simon sang, the cradle of the civil war 140 years previously, with two of its bloody campaigns around these mighty rivers. Of no less significance, during the second half of the twentieth century it was a hugely important centre of the human rights struggle towards race-equality both within and beyond the USA. Despite being part of such a young country, this region is steeped in history of huge global relevance.

Flying over this landscape of fertile soil with lots of water and trees makes any single-engine

Top: Checking position, south of Dallas
Above: The Mississippi river

aircraft pilot very aware of the possibility of an engine failure. There again, a lot of the surfaces I had overflown in the past month weren't exactly ideal for emergency landings either!

After passing Atlanta with its extremely busy airspace to the north of my track and 936nm (1,733km) from Abilene, I landed at the Savannah Hilton Head Airport having flown six hours and eighteen minutes to cover that distance. This had been a flight in great weather, and not even the initial strong southerly wind had any detrimental effect. In fact it gave me the benefit of a small tailwind component, which despite the very low power settings to which I had conditioned myself while crossing the vastness of the Pacific, contributed to a very pleasant average ground speed of 148.6kts (275kmh).

In common with most places on this fantastic journey, historic Savannah had a feeling all of its own and it was very obvious that I had arrived in the Deep South. However, despite it being a place that shouldn't be missed, I was going to have to limit myself to an overnight stop and forego all sightseeing. The instability of the weather further north demanded I didn't waste any opportunities for the forthcoming Atlantic crossing, particularly as there was a good chance of an early weather window for this last ocean flight. I just needed to get to Bangor without any further delays. What the Atlantic lacks in size in relation to the Pacific, it fully compensates through its many and complex weather systems.

My handling agent in Savannah arranged a room at the local Days Inn, a good modestly-priced chain of hotels I already knew from Guam, which suited my travelling needs. Its main attributes were reasonable rooms, good internet availability and a free shuttle service. Its major drawback was a mediocre self-service cold breakfast. This free shuttle also took me to a restaurant from another apparently well-known chain – I can't remember the name and I had never heard of it, a fact that astonished the driver being an 'alien' in the USA must have been enough reason to explain my total ignorance! Despite this, they served interesting regional food, gave good service and I certainly enjoyed it.

My now-obligatory call to FIC early in the morning to check the weather and 'notams' (notices to airmen) for the flight to Bangor 955nm (1,769km) away, confirmed good conditions all the way. I was also glad that there were no particular comments about the two very sensitive security areas around Washington and New York.

With the mapping and flight plans sorted out on the laptop, I went to reception to print them, only to find out that the hotel had problems with their computers and was not able to help. Once back at the airport, I discovered that the world's most ancient computer resided at the handling agent's office in Savannah! It took this 'steam-driven' machine about an hour-and-a-quarter to print three pages before crashing comprehensively. A trip to the local maintenance/flying school/pilot shop produced an IFR chart up to Washington and they were also good enough to print the necessary stuff for me, even if they only had a black and white printer. Computers were clearly not in high demand around there and unfortunately it must be said that VFR charts in black and white are not very useful.

Once checked out and installed in the cockpit, asking for the flight clearance didn't prompt the response I was hoping for and after a while it transpired that my flight plan had been lost. Eventually the control tower suggested I spoke directly to the FIR of Macon (they were close enough to be able to use the VHF radio on the ground) and I then managed to file another flight plan with them over the radio.

Once that was sorted, I was swiftly sent on my way down a taxiway to the hold for the active runway. It was actually a little too swift for my liking as I was placed just ahead of a C-130 Hercules military transport aircraft with a departing clearance identical to mine, only at a lower level. Clearly the Hercules could cope with my wake turbulence better than I could with theirs,

but having that huge aircraft with four huge propellers ready to chew up anything in their path only a few yards behind me was ever so slightly unsettling…

After take-off and once radio communications were handed over by the tower to the FIC, I was asked if I was familiar with the security arrangements around Washington in a tone I interpreted as meaning, 'you really wouldn't be so stupid as to fly this route without this information, would you?' I said yes, but having said so was stretching the truth a long way. I was actually hoping that things would become obvious as time went by and was working with the idea in mind that if I was going to be told to avoid something I would simply ask by how much I was required to turn while already turning. I hoped that this approach would keep me from finding out about the US military firepower. As I never caught a glimpse of an F-16 fighter, I later decided that all's well that ends well.

After Savannah I started to get new variations of my call sign from some ATC operators. A few addressed me as, "Canadian G-GDRV", to which I felt quite smug by correcting them by replying, "Negative Canadian, G-GDRV is a British aircraft".[16] There were also others that appeared not to be able to accept that there are aircraft registered in countries other than the US and insisted on calling me NG-GDRV.

Due to the delays trying to print documents and the flight plan fiasco, any thoughts of a small detour to overfly Kitty Hawk had to be ignored. I really felt that passing the nest of powered aviation and not actually seeing it was a great shame. When some five years previously I had started planning this circumnavigation, visiting Kitty Hawk was one of my original goals, but now time was not on my side. To make matters worse the barometric pressure was dropping fast with the implied approaching bad weather, so I really had to push on towards Bangor. In fact over this leg the atmospheric pressure dropped by 20mb/0.59in Hg. The standard atmospheric pressure is 1013mb (millibars) in metric or 29.92in Hg (inches of mercury). A drop of 20mb is roughly the difference on a barometer face between 'FAIR' and 'RAIN' – a very significant change towards bad weather in such a short space of time. This was a clear graphic measure of the severity of what lay ahead.

Opposite: The James river and the Atlantic
Above: Long Island

Soon after passing west abeam Kitty Hawk and crossing the James river in Virginia, I got my first view of the Atlantic Ocean since I had begun this journey. Looking at this body of water and being well aware that it was the last major barrier between me and home provoked a strange mixture of emotions.

Shortly after crossing the river, the exclusion zones around Washington appeared and I am pleased to say that they really didn't affect my progress by as much as I had feared. Maybe my eagerness to comply with ATC instructions showed I wasn't about to blow up the White House.

Despite these high security considerations, I still had occasion to admire Delaware Bay, regardless of the presence of a warship parked in the middle of the mouth of the Delaware river as a reality check. No one could forget the obsession with security in the George W. Bush led-USA and, what's worse, it can be contagious. I could swear that the ship's gun turrets were tracking me! I strongly disliked – and will always detest – this constant security fear. I witnessed this security fear highlighted in parts of the US by the misguided admiration and awe towards my route through the countries of the Middle East. If this is a generalised view, what is the chance for peace and understanding between the peoples of the world? Maybe compulsory round the world trips would do the trick…

After passing east abeam Washington, my track crossed the coast at a shallow angle over a few affluent-looking places with marinas full of up-market pleasure vessels. New York itself was a great view and a highlight of the journey, as I passed close enough to see Manhattan reasonably well, although too far for my simple digital camera to pick up. Much as I squinted, I could not see the Statue of Liberty, I suppose it's too small against the skyscrapers! Long Island was very pretty from the air and ATC of JFK Airport were not bothered with my presence right by their airspace. Considering New York was the worst hit city in the 9/11 attack, its airspace doesn't have any of the restrictions I found near Washington. If I was a cynical type I would put it down to the president not living close by...

After crossing the Long Island Sound, the terrain again changed dramatically. The forests full of fir-trees were the predominant feature, along with very cold-looking blue water lakes, all decidedly pretty in a northern kind of way. Due to the fresh north-easterly wind and an unstable atmosphere I had a very choppy ride along there, often bumpy enough not to be able to hold the camera long enough to take a picture.

Bangor came into view and I landed just ahead of a Citation business jet. As a British PPL it never ceases to amaze me how all the different types of traffic blend together in the US. Why not everywhere else? Despite high air traffic density it all interacts perfectly – a good demonstration of how well it can consistently be done.

I was directed to the GA parking area where tie-downs and ropes were provided in all parking spaces. This is a windy country and a cold country too, the 30ft (10m) pile of dirty snow in the middle of the apron testified to that. I booked in the reception office, a place that didn't seem to enjoy too many laughs and was occupied by some very stern-looking staff. Asking for my Royal Aero Club record cards to be stamped, they showed a hidden sense of humour as the imprint of the stamp read: 'Arrived alive BGR, City of Bangor.' It made me laugh.

After meeting an English ferry pilot who appeared to have fallen foul of the local law, we teamed up and went to the local FIC office to find out what the weather had in store for us. The ever efficient meteorologists confirmed that the conditions for the crossing to the Azores were looking favourable for an ocean crossing forty-eight hours later.

The local Days Inn sent a car to collect me and the subsequent short trip took me through a country with an obviously harsh climate, all the contours of the landscape were smoothed over by past glacial activity and the squat, almost windowless buildings indicated hard winters still present to this day.

The restaurant next to the hotel was good enough despite its fortress-like unfriendly outside appearance. After enjoying a pleasant dinner I decided to take a stroll along the road to buy snacks for the next flight from the general store at a petrol filling station. This night walk on an unlit road was an excellent demonstration of a country that doesn't give a lot of thought to the possibility of pedestrians – but as there are so few, I suppose it doesn't really matter.

So after successfully managing not to get run over by the huge trucks thundering past, I got back to my room in a fairly relaxed frame of mind and ready for a good sleep.

Chapter 19
BANGOR TO HALIFAX

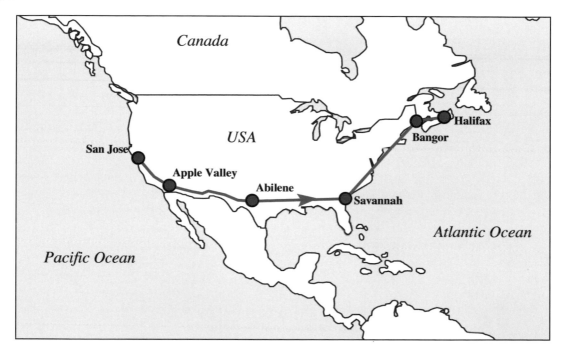

While trying to make the best of a poor breakfast selection, I again met Geoff Hall, the English ferry pilot I had come across the previous evening. Geoff, one of aviation's many colourful characters, came originally from Yorkshire but was now living in Florida and his work as a ferry pilot involves delivering new aircraft to their owners all over the world. We decided to team up for the day as it is always good to bounce ideas off somebody else 'in the same boat' and there was always a chance that two brains might be better than one.

The hotel's shuttle service got us back to the FIC office at the airport where we had a long chat with the duty officer about the weather conditions to cross the Atlantic. The preferred route via St Johns was still going to be out of the question for the foreseeable future due to a 200ft cloud base and freezing rain, not to mention the strong headwinds further east on the way to Greenland and Iceland, the more conventional route for light aircraft across the North Atlantic.

My own preferred route direct to Ireland was also not feasible for the same reason. The alternative of going further south via Santa Maria in the Azores was looking promising for the following night, or the day after that. The problem with this route was that the wind in Santa Maria seemed unlikely to slow down to a reasonable level, or for that matter turn into a direction reasonably close to the runway alignment. On the positive side and according to the published airfield map, there were a couple of disused runways of unknown condition that might be of some help should I get into any trouble. And there was always the fact that the Azores have many airport-equipped islands, the nearest one to Santa Maria was São Miguel, only 53nm (98km) away with a runway better suited to a westerly wind.

Armed with this information, we sat down for some serious planning. Why were we trying so hard to get to Santa Maria? After all, this is the most eastern island of the Azores archipelago, therefore the furthest from Bangor, actually 2,010nm (3,722km), against 1,690nm (3,130km) to Flores, the most western island. The reason was the availability of Avgas, all the other islands only had Jet fuel, which was of no use to either of our aircraft. Because of G-RV's huge endurance, going directly to Santa Maria from Bangor was quite feasible for me. However for Geoff with the Cessna 172 he was delivering to Germany, it would have been very marginal, despite having an enormous ferry tank where the rear seats used to be.

As the weather window for the crossing of the Atlantic was still at least a day away, we decided to use the available time to reduce the ocean crossing distance with a short repositioning flight. To that effect Geoff was going to fly to Sydney that afternoon (not Australia of course). This was Sydney in Nova Scotia, which was as far north as he could go before hitting the bad weather. As distance was not such an issue for me, I decided to go the following day to Halifax, the capital of Nova Scotia, where I expected to find better facilities.

To make sure everything was well for the following day's flight, I went over to check the aircraft and was unhappy with a small leak from the starboard brake. I had already spotted this in Savannah the previous day and had decided then it wasn't important, but now I felt it would be foolish to ignore it. Telford Aviation, the local maintenance organisation, were most accommodating and keen to help. Not only were they quick and able, but they were also commendably inexpensive.

Now that the brakes were being fixed, I felt much happier and a lot more confident to tackle the cross-wind in the Azores. Particularly as the forecast indicated I was going to have to deal with a north-westerly flow, potentially requiring lots of use from the starboard brake upon landing in Santa Maria.

While idly watching the engineer at work and as the weather was never very far from my thoughts in Bangor, I couldn't help being impressed by the amount of insulation all over the hangar – even the doors had a foot thick of heat insulation. Bangor can obviously be seriously cold, despite being at the same latitude as Bordeaux.

In the evening I had the opportunity to enjoy a chowder in the restaurant that looked like (and I suppose it was) a fortress against the cold. Chowder, a thick, chunky seafood soup from North America is believed to have originated in French Canada and has made its way down the coast to New England. I certainly found it most enjoyable. Later on I went back to my navigation and worked out the possible routes back home via the Azores with the aid of the FlightStar software.

The next morning started a lot better than when I previously left Savannah. Despite this particular hotel also not having a customer-usable printer, the manageress was kind enough to print my charts and navigation logs in her office and I found myself at the airfield checking the aircraft without any undue delays. While finishing my external checks, yet another ferry pilot from Yorkshire, David, came over to say hello. David was also delivering a new Cessna 172, although this one was going to Barcelona. It seemed that Bangor was a gateway for ferry pilots setting off across the Atlantic.

As it appeared they were clearing customs on leaving the US, I decided to do the same and not miss any less obvious procedure. It has to be said I didn't enjoy my ensuing visit to the US customs in Bangor. They showed a great deal of suspicion towards my unusual flight and I was questioned in a fairly unpleasant manner, until they realised I wasn't a latter day incarnation of Al Capone. I eventually worked out that the others were simply going to customs because they were exporting US-registered aircraft, which of course I wasn't.

Upon starting up, the attitude indicator (AI) wobbled in a sick sort of way. This was something new and most undesirable as this gyroscopic equipment is the primary instrument for flight without visual references, making it hugely important. I considered going back to Telford Aviation and asking them to replace it as they were the best and cheapest people to get such a task carried out, but as the AI sorted itself out quickly I decided against it. This decision turned out to haunt me.

The short flight of only 226nm (419 km) from Bangor to Halifax was quite uneventful and, similarly to the flight into Bangor the previous day, it also gave a choppy ride. As time wasn't an issue and this was the shortest international flight of the whole adventure, I decided to stay low and slow to enjoy the view.

Once again the experience of sitting in the most wonderful royal box with the world going by underneath brought back to me the realisation of just how privileged I was simply being able to fly and savour all these sights usually denied to ground-bound beings.

The passing landscape was of a very obviously northern nature and consisted of dense woods crossed and dotted by water in the form of rivers and lakes. Of these sights, two things struck me: one was the lines of dead trees following the water courses and the other was the straight lines of cleared trees running through the forests. At first I mistook the latter for firebreaks and therefore good potential emergency landing places, however the majority of these tree-less lines were not firebreaks, but were in fact forestry clearances for power lines with huge electricity pylons – not a good place to try to land! As to the cause of the dead trees along the water courses I wasn't too sure. Could it have been beavers chewing around the trees?

Halifax has quite a large international airport and it looked as if it might be as cold as Bangor. On second thoughts, once I looked at the big chunks of snow left by the snowploughs, I thought it may well be even colder.

The people in the Shell/IMP company who were handling my flight were very helpful and went about their business in what I thought was a more English or European manner, much in contrast with those just the other side of the border. This was easier to sense than explain. I had all the fuel tanks filled up to the top and arranged to be back there around 3.00 a.m. local time to cross the Atlantic to the Azores. The very helpful lady in reception arranged a room at the local Hilton, only about four miles away and operating a free shuttle service.

Once in the hotel, I decided to have dinner quite early in order to maximise my sleeping and resting time before the long haul of 1,783nm (3,302km) to the Azores. On my way to the restaurant I again met Yorkshireman David and his American friend James. It turned out that they were travelling together as they were delivering not just one, but two new Cessna 172s to Barcelona. They were also going to Santa Maria in the early hours, so we all had dinner together and were soon joined by a flying folded-newspaper hitting James fully on the chest and heralding the arrival of Denny Craig. Denny was a fantastically colourful individual, having flown B52s and the like in Vietnam, certainly not averse to picking a good row and possibly a fight to complement it. He was a great connoisseur of the Manila delights, probably had a zillion flying hours to his credit and had seen and done it all! Denny was delivering a Beech Bonanza to Africa. It was simply fascinating to be surrounded by what, for me, was a most unusual set of people – I

CHASING THE MORNING SUN

suppose that sort of job over a long time requires an unusual sort of person. These guys had an amazing amount of experience and a lot of attitude.

We were all going to leave that night for Santa Maria. A most interesting evening and a good way of dispelling any wishes I may have had of becoming a ferry pilot.

Despite the booked alarm call never materialising, I was up at 1.45 a.m. local, after quite a good rest, if not much sleep. Coffee and some sort of 'plastic food' for breakfast (the hotel couldn't provide a packed breakfast) proved that there are times when it might be better to go hungry! Suffering from the aftertaste of this food substitute and after a long wait for the shuttle bus, I finally got to the airport which was completely deserted except for the guy on night duty.

Once the pre-flight checks were completed and as this flight was going to take place over the cold waters of the Atlantic, it was time to get into the immersion suit that I had been carrying in the back of the aircraft since Abilene. This would give me a fighting chance of survival if I ended up in the water. The suit threw up a few problems I hadn't anticipated. First of all I had to transfer all the bits I was going to need during the flight from the numerous pockets of my flying suit into a single small sleeve-pocket in the immersion suit, leaving quite a lot in need of a home somewhere within arm's reach in the cockpit. The other problem became obvious as I was getting myself into the immersion suit and doing up its waterproof zip. The whole thing was trapping air inside and I felt like a passable caricature of the Michelin man. This was, of course due to the suit being rubberised with integral rubber boots and very efficient seals around the wrists and neck, in fact the latter was oppressively tight. There was no remedy for the tightness of the neck seal – but I found that the way to deflate the suit was to roll myself into a ball while holding the neck seal slightly open with my fingers – good job there were no onlookers!

After getting myself back into the cockpit and sorting all my leftover bits and pieces into a variety of locations around the place, it was time to start up. At this point and to my dismay, the AI was once again not erecting, most probably because the gyro was not spinning fast enough to work correctly. I tried revving up, waiting for a time, shutting down and restarting, taxiing around a bit, but nothing – it just wouldn't do more than wobble around and, unlike the last time in Bangor, it wouldn't correct itself. The prospect of missing the obvious window to Santa Maria was pretty depressing, but the possibility of starting a flight in conditions where IMC was likely seemed pretty stupid. So kicking myself for not having had it sorted out in Bangor, I had to call it a day and parked up again just in time to see my ferry pilot friends arriving and getting ready to go. Both the Cessna 172s left soon after, but Denny with the Bonanza had a bad fuel leak from the ferry tank and was only able to leave later in the morning after an engineer had worked on it for a few hours.

The local avionics shop was located in a part of the hangar of IMP, so it was a question of hanging around until they opened for business. This turned out to be a long wait in the early hours, culminating with the arrival of the most unfriendly receptionist in the whole of Canada. When the avionics shop did open, things didn't look much better as they didn't have an AI of any sorts, and the prospect of having one ordered from Ontario with the weekend almost upon us was not appealing. The possibility of returning to Bangor to get Telford Aviation to sort it out at possibly cheaper (US) prices wasn't really on the cards either as all fuel tanks were absolutely full to the brim and a grossly overweight landing was not recommended. Eventually a second-hand unit was located at some other organisation in the airport, for which they wanted Can$1,200, making it more expensive than a brand new unit in the USA!

As I wasn't prepared to consider losing another possibility, however tenuous, of a weather window to cross the Atlantic, I accepted the asking price. Not only the price of the unit, but also the work to make an adapter for the panel as the two casings were different. The work started well enough, but the actual instrument installation quickly degenerated into a ridiculous performance with me ending up fitting and removing the unit several times into the panel. We eventually got it sorted out before closing time and it actually worked as it should, which was

quite a surprise. By then the nice receptionist was back at her desk and she reserved me another room at the Garden Hilton.

So there I was, stuck once again waiting for a weather window. Clearly the only thing to do was to go and see the countryside in that part of the world. After all I knew nothing about it and I hadn't planned to visit it, so this was the opportunity to correct that gap in my knowledge. To do that I needed a car and the following day, Thursday, I went to the air-

Waiting for a weather window in Halifax International

port terminal to be pleasantly surprised at how inexpensive hire cars were in Nova Scotia. A huge Ford 4x4 was just too tempting at those prices, so I hired one, only to discover very quickly that the advertised price in Canada is before taxes and things like insurance, making the final price around twice the advertised price – you live and learn!

With the brand new Ford Expedition giving me a new freedom, my first port of call was the local FIC office. This was actually sited in the airport but accessed from a remote track and it was clear they didn't get many visitors. The people there were most helpful and they were at least as good as their American colleagues – they provided a splendid service. Regrettably the forecast wasn't as good as I might have wished for and it appeared that a window before Tuesday was most unlikely. It must be said that there was a slim chance for Sunday, but it didn't look too promising. To finish my visit there I was given a tour of their most impressive facilities and saw the pictures of all the grounded and parked up aircraft on 9/11, with every bit of the airport covered in airliners except for the one runway   it was an incredible sight.

I went to have a look around Halifax and Dartmouth and had lunch in a nice little restaurant in Dartmouth where I had the best sea-food chowder I've ever tasted, with at least half a lobster in it – wow! This restaurant was in a shopping mall that was clearly built to survive the extreme cold that their winters can bring. It was here that I first heard of the Juno festival of music and the impact it has in Halifax. I was in no doubt that this was the one occasion when Halifax becomes the focal point of international attention.

On a more practical note, I was also told about Peggy's Cove as an especially beautiful coastal place to visit. As the distance from Dartmouth to Peggy's Cove was about a couple of inches on the map from Hertz, I decided (without knowing the scale) to go and have a look. The landscape was certainly interesting, windswept, rugged – and far! The actual village and its main attraction, the lighthouse, was worth a visit. The wilderness of the terrain carved by glaciers, the wild sea and the powerful wind amounted to a great experience. However the whole trip, including returning to the hotel, totalled around 130 miles.

As feared, the window for Sunday never materialised, I went off to explore more of Halifax. First I went across from Dartmouth to Halifax on the ferry and had a look at the seafront and the most interesting Maritime Museum of the Atlantic. With its geographical position, the history of Halifax

is obviously interconnected with sea travel and all its implications. The sinking of the Titanic occurred just 650nm (1,200km) away from Halifax, and to this day there are all manner of relics from that ill-fated liner in the museum. Many of the fatalities of that disaster are buried in Halifax.

Another unusual aspect of the museum is the exhibition dedicated to the Halifax explosion of 6th December 1917, which was the biggest man-made explosion before the atomic bomb. This was caused by a collision between two ships, one of them full of explosives, which flattened much of Halifax, shattering windows fifty miles away and instantly killing nearly 2,000 people.

Later, I returned to Halifax by road and went to the Halifax Citadel, a splendid fort of British origin which was immaculately preserved, but not fully open as the tourist season was yet to start.

Both in Halifax proper and at the airport I found plenty of evidence of the Juno festival in the form of outside broadcast vehicles and an astonishing number of business jets delivering all manner of apparently famous people. I remember having a group called Coldplay pointed out to me by an over-excited young lady – shame I had never heard of them before! There were many others, but they didn't mean a thing to me and, unlike Coldplay, didn't have a name I could link with music and cold weather, so I promptly forgot them…

Sometime during the weekend and because I had plenty of time to waste on the internet, I read an air-worthiness directive (AD) on the Vans website. It required checking the fuel tanks and their pick-up pipes before the next flight.[17] This was somewhat alarming, as I was about to set off across the Atlantic Ocean! After calming down, I recollected that the port main tank wasn't affected by that particular problem and I thought that the starboard tank had a similar arrangement, but as I couldn't be absolutely 100% certain, I decided that leaving a good reserve of fuel in the forward tank would be a good insurance policy. Monday was a day to be optimistic about the weather. Upon checking the aeroplane it was evident that it had been venting quite a lot of fuel from the main tanks. This is a shortcoming of the system as it wasn't designed to have all the tanks full over a long period of time while sitting unused on the ground. It turned out that it lost 20lt over the five days that it was parked in Halifax.

Full of optimism about the weather forecast, I returned the Ford to the hire company.

Once again I re-calculated the route to the Azores; the weather window was there, but inevitably it was not as good as it had looked a few days beforehand. I planned a departure going

Opposite: A ferry between Halifax and Dartmouth
Above: A waterside view of Halifax

well south of the GC track to avoid and take advantage of the low pressure system just east of Halifax. The cold front that was trundling to the Azores needed a large amount of consideration, and crossing it at the 40° north parallel looked a good compromise between avoiding icing to the north and embedded CBs to the south. The METAR report for Santa Maria was giving a wind of 25kt, gusting 35kt from 90° to the left, but the TAF forecast allowed a degree of optimism, with the wind due to veer by some 40° and slowing to 15kt.

There was an element of déjà vu with the rest of the day and evening. The tanks were topped up just before departure and I also de-iced the wings with the correct fluid, a pretty common occurrence around there. Taxiing out I was anxious to make sure everything was working as intended. It was, and it felt good to be finally on the move after my previous failures.

Chapter 20
HALIFAX TO SANTA MARIA

The take-off from a heavily-frosted Halifax into the pitch-black night restarted the series of long-range flights that were at the heart of this adventure. Soon after I left the shores of the North American continent for good, although I never actually saw the coast line. In this thinly-populated area there are simply not enough lights to mark the dividing line between land and sea.

I had learnt during the course of these flights that switching on the taxi light was the easiest way to check if I had gone into cloud. So once again I did just that and briefly wondered whether I could possibly have entered the clearest atmosphere ever, as nothing at all appeared in the beam of light. However I hadn't entered a vacuum and had to accept that the light had failed. I found this exceedingly irritating, after all the waiting of the previous five days and the technical problem that caused it in the first place, I wasn't in the mood for more headaches. Worse still, there were good reasons to worry about it. Firstly, if I was to arrive in Santa Maria after sunset, the subsequent taxiing without that light was going to be very difficult, especially if I didn't have the benefit of a 'Follow Me' truck to lead me away from the runway. Although there was a high probability of this happening, the consequences were more inconvenient than terrifying – however, if I was to find myself needing to ditch into the sea in the dark and not have the taxi light to help me judge the last few feet to the surface, that would be a very different story.

The 4th April dawned bright and beautiful with the temperature above freezing and the cold waters of the North Atlantic giving the sort of background that, although not actually friendly, did not seem particularly threatening either. Maybe the combination of the reassuring purr of the Lycoming engine and the sunshine had a lot to do with this.

However, the weather didn't remain like that for long, the temperature slowly dropped and cloud started to form at the lower levels as had been forecast. At first only as a few dotted small cumulus and strato-cumulus, but it then progressively increased to a full cover over the ocean. The flight conditions were nonetheless very good for several hours and I found it was quite easy to settle into my ocean crossing routine with one exception: the design of the immersion suit made calls of nature much more awkward than normal. How long distance female pilots cope with it, I'll never know! The required undoing of the unyielding immersion suit zip with an opening not designed for that purpose and fastening it up again was not easy, but at least the auto-pilot did a splendid job of 'minding the shop' while I was otherwise occupied! To generally simplify the procedure, I found it was easier not to bother to do up the flying suit underneath – little did I know how this was going to have an unexpected result later on.

The relaxed progress of the flight was rudely jolted by the 'new' AI starting to tilt into a right bank for no good reason. This bank went on increasing until it got to 90°, indicating a complete failure of the unit. This also caused a complete failure of my sense of humour and then got much worse. The three gyroscopic instrument set provides the only means of executing a flight away from visual references and the AI is the most important instrument within that set. This was very bad.

For the multitude of questions invading my mind I was having a real problem finding any answers. How was I going to cope with a partially-failed panel for the next nine hours? What if another gyro failed? Should I go back and land in guaranteed daylight? What if the weather coming from the west was to arrive in Halifax before I got back? Was I prepared to waste yet another weather window? What about the cold front that was lying ahead? What about the al-most overwhelming blinding anger urging me to go back to Halifax and do something unmen-tionable with the failed gyro? All these problems and thoughts created one of the highest levels of anxiety I had ever experienced in my life.

It is on occasions like these that we are confronted with our inner selves, without any outside influences. There is a lot to learn in a very short time, including a great deal that is going to be unacceptable to our egos. One of the things I learnt was that the more time I had to think about the correct decision involving my own survival, the more difficult it was to reach that decision. And as I had lots of time – the current conditions weren't presenting an immediate danger – it was agonisingly difficult. This is the complete opposite of reacting to emergency situations in an instinctive or trained manner, where there is an automatic process that can be put into action. In this case I had to analyse and weigh all the factors against one another in order to come up with the best solution for what ultimately could be the difference between my life and death.

These considerations vividly highlighted the essence of the purely solo flight over huge dis-tances, echoing the type of adventure that the pioneers of the golden age of aviation must have experienced. The buck stops here in the cockpit, all the decisions and their consequences are the pilot's – mine – and nobody else's. There was no possibility of satellite telephone conferences with backing teams, no possibility of asking for advice or even simple reassurance. I was well and truly on my own.

However, although the initial horror and anger had inevitably concentrated my mind on the restrictive and negative aspects of my situation, once that anxiety could be tamed I was back in control. The bigger picture could be assessed and common sense prevailed once again! I sup-pose one of the greatest achievements of an individual is to overcome his or her own fears and shortcomings. How I actually got there is a moot point, but the absolute need to reach a work-able decision must have had a lot to do with it.

In this newly-found positive frame of mind, I was able to make the decision to carry on to-wards the Azores. To help reduce the possibility of 'the leans' and general annoyance, I taped a piece of card over the instrument, a normal practice in such circumstances as it is far better not to have an instrument at all than to have one that is giving an incorrect display,

After a couple of hours of cooling down and getting used to the new situation, I noticed through a small gap in the improvised AI covering that there was a change in its display. And by removing the cover completely I found a 30° bank in the opposite direction. As the weather at the time was good VMC I decided to leave it uncovered to check for any further change, and to my astonishment after about one hour it regained a near correct indication. Carrying out a few high bank turns and fairly steep pitch angle changes confirmed that it was functioning rea-sonably well with a small list to port, so I decided to leave it uncovered and cautiously use it as a working but unreliable instrument.

A few hours later, New York radio passed a request from Santa Maria ATC for me to climb to FL120 before entering their zone, to which I had to reply I was unable to comply due to lack of oxygen and de-icing facilities. As Santa Maria was adamant I was going to have to fly at that level because of their mountains, requests and answers went back and forwards in a flurry for a while. As the highest peak in the Azores is the extinct volcano of Pico at around 7,500ft and is restricted horizontally by the island only being 25nm (46km) long by 8nm (15km) wide, I thought such a demand unreasonable and unnecessary. Thankfully they eventually dropped the request.

After passing some lines of deep clouds and just about to consider myself lucky for finding the cold front as a reasonably weak event, I reached the main part of the system! As I couldn't outclimb the huge clouds and to avoid another icing episode, I had to descend to a lower level due to the large temperature drop when not in direct view of the sun. At the same time I was handed over from New York HF radio to Santa Maria HF radio, so I requested a change of level as a consequence of my potential icing problem. Their apparent apathy was spotted by New York radio who were still following my progress and in no uncertain terms conveyed the urgency of my request. This was the second time in this adventure that an American HF operator had intervened on my behalf when another country's operator didn't seem to fully understand their safety role. I can't really say that Santa Maria rushed to respond, so I went along with their time scale and tailored reports accordingly.

With around one hour to go before Flores, the first island of the archipelago, a new clearance was issued to route via the north of the islands, therefore increasing the total distance substantially. When I questioned the reason for that clearance, I was astonished to hear the old argument of the height of the mountain being brought back. This sounded to me particularly unreasonable as the direct route from my current position to the island was clear of the islands to the south, and actually crossing the islands to the north didn't seem to be the best way to avoid the mountains. Finally they saw sense and they retracted the disputed clearance.

The actual islands were mostly covered in cloud, including the volcano in Pico. The only exceptions were the island of Flores that I could see reasonably well under its own cloud and the distant island of São Miguel that for a short time revealed a volcanic form sticking out from its cloud cover.

Santa Maria itself allowed glimpses of the airport, but most of the island, which rises sharply to the east, was covered in cloud. As at the time they didn't have their newly-installed radar fully operational, I didn't have my hoped-for vectored approach. When considering the proximity of the high ground I elected to carry out the VOR procedure to runway 36, resulting in a delay long enough to miss landing in daylight. The combination of a wind of over 40kt and some very black clouds meant I performed an interestingly-shaped procedure.

The forthcoming landing started to look ominous as soon as I was established on final and was visual with runway 36. With an airspeed of just over 100kt I was looking at the runway through the right-hand side of the windscreen, certainly further off-centre than I had ever seen a runway on a final approach in this aeroplane. As ATC was giving a surface wind from 290° between 20 and 25kt (and knowing the reputation of the place for crosswinds) I thought it was only fair to inform ATC that those conditions were right on the limit of the aircraft. Reducing speed to the middle of the white arc and not deploying flap, gave an athletic approach to the runway with the stick going around all four corners of the cockpit.[18] The ASI needle was flailing by some 20kt and a stiff right leg forced the rudder into its stop. That wasn't quite enough to line up the aircraft with the runway and a number of tries went on for most of its length of 3,000m. Upon abandoning the landing run and declaring I was going around, I was asked by the ATC lady to state my intentions. I managed to avoid saying "honourable" and just squeaked, "a landing would be nice". I don't think she was amused.

In the following downwind leg, I had time to rest my right leg and consider my options: a) the disused runways were of no use at all as by now it was completely dark; b) although the cross-wind component was fairly constant throughout the length of the runway, the turbulence created by the adjacent 300ft cliff was not as bad at the threshold as it was over the rest of it and it could be worth aiming for that; c) all else failing, I still had plenty of fuel and the alternative in São Miguel, 53nm (98km) away might be an option as the runway was orientated more into wind, although the mountain next to it was not in its favour. I decided to go for the second option.

So the next time I was pointing at the runway, I concentrated on landing at the very beginning of it, with half-flap set and well aware that the insurance company might not like the result. This time it worked and I was glad to be on *terra firma* and in one piece. It had taken me twelve hours and forty-six minutes to cover the GC distance of 1,783nm (3,302km) from Halifax to these islands, the most western part of Portugal and of the European Union. The actual flown distance was 1,900nm (3,519km).

A call to ATC produced a 'Follow Me' vehicle to meet me at the holding point. This turned out to be of no help. Upon meeting he immediately proceeded to race back to the terminal as fast as he could, leaving me to pick my own way without a taxi light.

Eventually I reached the very wide and windy apron with no tie-downs which made parking there completely out of the question. While 'Speedy' went to see if the maintenance hangar could be used to keep the aircraft overnight, I was met by António Pacheco, the local Portuguese television (RTP) correspondent. He was also the meteorological officer at the airport with whom I had exchanged emails regarding my passage through the Azores, and his wish to interview me. Although it was too dark to film my multiple arrivals, I understand that listening to bursts of tyre squeals progressing up the runway had been very entertaining.

Once in the hangar, I could relax regarding the safety of the aircraft and pose with various dignitaries and enthusiasts for photographs. With the television camera already rolling, I took off the immersion suit before the interview as it was quite uncomfortable and I thought it might help me to look a little more awake, despite being undeniably tired. It was only some way through the interview that I noticed the lower zip of my flying suit wide open, as it had been for the last nine hours or so. If anybody else noticed, they were too polite to mention it – I just hope the shots were close enough to only show my head and upper torso!

The airport maintenance manager was kind enough to give me a lift to the Santa Maria Hotel, arriving there just before the restaurant closing time.

The hotel was built in a former American air force base and although it had an appearance reminiscent of the sixties, I believe it had been rebuilt since then and it was pleasant and airy enough. Possibly too airy for the time of the year! It also seemed strangely deserted but that impression might have been caused by the late hour of my arrival.

The restaurant staff couldn't have been more helpful, despite my arrival making them unduly late to finish work. It felt quite odd to be in a restaurant with Portuguese food and language in the middle of all my travels. The food was certainly very tasty, but not having had proper food for more than twenty-four hours makes anyone's taste buds appreciative.

The room was not untypical of budget summer resorts of a few decades ago, with thin walls, cheap decoration and no heater. Despite that, it had a pleasant feel and the old fashioned Lusitanian heavy blanket in the cupboard was certainly most appreciated.

In the morning I found the hotel's restaurant busy serving breakfast, dispelling my previous day's thoughts that I was the only guest staying there. I was glad to see that the helpfulness and friendliness of the staff had not suffered from the extra workload and it was equally obvious that I must have been the attraction of the year! Such an attitude went a long way to show that this small island has limited entertainment.

While battling with the reception's ancient printer for my usual flight papers and chasing interconnecting cables with the help of the receptionist, another member of the staff congratulated me on my command of the Portuguese language, which I had to admit was hardly surprising, as it was my native tongue! After the ensuing embarrassment on her part and my vain attempts at making light of it, once I found myself on my own, I had to wonder if I was in danger of becoming a full-time outsider. Since leaving Portugal over thirty years ago, I have never been concerned about losing my Portuguese accent when speaking English. I have however, unwittingly acquired an English accent when speaking Portuguese and as my French had been neglected for so long, it has been contaminated by an Anglo-Portuguese accent. Could I become a sort of a linguistic 'Flying Dutchman' doomed to sail (or fly) the oceans forever, never finding a home port? Thankfully however, these gloomy thoughts were soon dispelled because, to continue the analogy, and if the Wagnerian version of this legend is anything to go by, I must have been already 'saved' by the love of a faithful woman and I know beyond doubt that England is now my home.

Although I had doubts about the availability of taxis in Santa Maria, I didn't have to worry about finding transport as the hotel was keen on giving me a lift to the airport in the van that was about to do the shopping rounds. Once there I had to blag my way to airside (easier than in most places) and then find the Met Office where once again I met António Pacheco as well as his sister Alexandra, who was also a meteorologist. Looking at the available information, we could see that the weather wasn't looking too good in the Azores area and it was appalling around the island. I felt that there was an inclination to dissuade me to depart that day and as the weather I could see out of the window was very miserable, it wasn't too difficult to allow myself to be persuaded to stay another day. After all, the world record was no longer a possibility and I wasn't that keen on fighting bad weather once more without a very good reason.

When António asked me for a longer interview I did wonder, following the previous evening's dressing incident, if he simply needed to re-record a broadcastable version. As well as the interview, I had my photo taken with people who were kind enough to make a televised formal gift presentation to mark my passage through Santa Maria. I was quite worried about the weight of those gifts and how I could explain the difficulty of fitting everything in the plane without upsetting anybody. Although it took me a while, I eventually worked out that the long sea crossings were already behind me and I could afford to accommodate a few extra pounds of weight, a new and strange concept.

António turned out to be the perfect host and not only insisted that I stayed overnight at his house, but also took the day off work to show me around the island. While he went to attend to the details of these unscheduled plans, I went to check the aircraft and visited the ops room to enquire if G-RV could remain in the maintenance hangar for another twenty-four hours. Although they were happy to oblige, they were simultaneously showing undue concern for having to charge me for an additional day and profusely apologised for not being able to avoid that charge. With memories of the outrageous charges in Manila flooding back, I summoned the most unperturbed tone of voice I could manage and enquired about the likely cost. After a lot of searching through many filing cabinets and my expectations growing darker with every consulted file, the answer came back as a whopping €3 a night! I accepted that with great relief.

The way back to the Met Office from the ops room was through a long corridor decorated with a collection of splendid black and white photographs of aircraft visiting throughout its history. I thought the most memorable pictures were the ones of two Concordes together, an Airbus Beluga and a turbine-equipped DC3. By the time I got back we had been joined by Tomás, António's eighteen-month-old son, and the three of us headed out for an island tour.

António proved to be an excellent guide, starting by showing me the volcanic and sedimen-

tary geological structure of the island, a fact easily observed where the new roads had cut through the hills. This is curiously in contrast with all the other exclusively volcanic islands in the Azores and is because Santa Maria is geologically much older than its neighbours.

Soon after our departure I had to wonder about the accuracy of the weather forecasts, despite my meteorologist guide. When I had first arrived at the airfield that morning, the fog was so bad we could not see across the width of the runway. Less than half an hour after starting our trip I couldn't see a single cloud in the sky. On the positive side, fog is no good for sightseeing either and the dramatic improvement in the weather was most welcome because Santa Maria is exceedingly pretty, and surprisingly diverse considering it is only 9nm east-west by 5nm north-south (17km by 9km). The various bays and hills are beautifully distinct from each other and display a sub-tropical vegetation that adds to their exoticism.

A special point of interest in the villages we drove through was that the great majority of houses are uncannily similar to the typical houses of southern continental Portugal – a consequence of the majority of the population originating from those areas. This does not mean they are recent villages, they can and often do go back several centuries. The island was one of the first lands to be discovered by Portuguese ships and was charted in 1427. Just like the rest of the Azores, Santa Maria was unpopulated before the Portuguese got there, but it soon received its first settlers in the form of whole families and their cattle, presumably to support future nautical expeditions. Most of these houses are whitewashed with the corners painted in a colour signifying an allegiance to their parish or to the parish where their inhabitants originated from.

Despite their immaculate condition, a high percentage of the villages are almost deserted. The majority of houses belonged to emigrants who have moved, mostly to the USA or Canada, leaving no one behind. António told me they are kept in such good order because they have been retained as holiday houses by their generally successful owners in their new lives abroad. It appears that some of those still living in the villages have found occupation by becoming caretakers for the empty houses. These villages look extremely appealing to anyone willing to travel in search of the ultimate destination to get away from it all, and certainly from the hustle

Top: Hosts António and Tomás Pacheco
Above: The author enjoying the view above São Lourenço

A typical Santa Maria bay

and bustle of the big cities. Such a traveller would also be rewarded with ornithological opportunities as well as numerous sightings of dolphins and whales swimming very close to the coast. The presence of the latter would be of no surprise to those familiar with the history of the Azores, once an important whaling centre. A further attraction of the island to those arriving by air is of course the likelihood of an exciting landing – admittedly not a point universally appreciated.

After the comprehensive tour of the island we went back to António's house where I had the opportunity to meet his charming wife and teenage daughter. In the evening we were invited to his sister Alexandra's for a BBQ, where we were joined by their mother, also a meteorologist, albeit retired – this profession is obviously a family trait!

This was a very pleasant occasion with a beautiful meal of freshly caught fish, as is appropriate to a small island in the middle of the Atlantic away from all forms of pollution.

Chapter 21
SANTA MARIA TO CASCAIS

With my sightseeing interlude over, the following morning started by going back to do battle with the weather charts at the airport. The weather around the island was decidedly better than the day before, although the low pressure system with lots of rain and embedded CBs was now sitting on my track to Lisbon. A dog-leg towards Madeira for 270nm (500km) followed by a direct track to Lisbon's GA airfield in Cascais looked like a reasonable solution to avoid the worst of the storm. All that remained was to calculate the finer points, file a flight plan, refuel and I would be ready to go. Filing the flight plan was not easy as there was a new computer system in operation with which my plan didn't conform, but they eventually got it sorted out and I was ready to depart.

Just before carrying out my pre-flight checks, I managed to get a ride with an airport official to satisfy my curiosity and see if the disused runways would in fact have been a viable proposition in an emergency. The 04/22 runway appeared to have quite a good surface, but it had lights across it in two places as part of the edge lighting of the 18/36 runway. These lights looked very solid and were about eight inches tall, so not a good place to land. The surface of the other runway, roughly orientated 15/33, was very poor and was also equipped with identical lights, therefore even less suitable for landing. It was just as well I didn't have the opportunity to attempt that option.

The way Santa Maria ATC insists on handling the departure clearance puts into action their cunning plan to ensure aircraft crossing the Atlantic have an operational HF radio set. This is revealed by their absolute refusal to issue the clearance in VHF, something I had learnt from previous long-distance flyers. Only once the clearance is sorted in HF is the departing aircraft handed back to normal VHF procedures prior to taxiing out.

The wind was from 220° direction and with a speed of 18kt, which prompted a start for the take-off roll from the left side of the runway to allow a diagonal displacement to the right on the ground run to slightly reduce the crosswind component. As it happened it wasn't needed, so it all went well and without any drama, a great improvement on my dramatic arrival.

Heading in the direction of Madeira to skirt around the low pressure system and towards the pressure trough that I was going to have to cross, as soon as I reached my cruising level I had the first mini-drama. This manifested itself as a severe engine misfire upon reducing power at the top of the climb. Resuming full power made the engine run smoothly again and backing the power once more had the opposite effect. As always the prospect of a ditching was terrifying! While considering how to get back to the runway safe and dry, the penny dropped – I had coarsely leaned out the carburettor mixture too much and changing the throttle setting induced the misfire. Once the mixture was correctly set all was well. Sub-consciously I must have considered that a sea crossing of only 800nm (1,482km) was going to be short and easy, not requiring the thorough preparation I always carried out, a singularly stupid attitude. A definite case of the six Ps: Poor Preparation Precedes Pretty Poor Performance, or some such words! Lapses of concentration and attention to detail like this have been known to kill people.

The promised bad weather of the trough wasn't as bad as I had had to deal with on previous occasions, so it was not too difficult to keep clear of icing and it only took around thirty minutes to cross. The skies then cleared into a beautiful blue, and I had to act with some restraint not to turn towards Lisbon earlier than in my calculated plan. It was just as well I stuck to my route as later on I passed a lot of bad weather to port and it was then clear that if I had given into that temptation and cut the corner, I would have gone through the middle of the storm.

I thought the HF service from Santa Maria could have been a lot better, just as I had on my way there. I got the impression that they were being plain lazy and didn't wish to have to struggle with a less than ideal radio reception, including appearing to be too keen on passing me onto VHF, irrespective of service availability in that band.

During one of our last communications the fuel tank in use ran out completely. I had been too distracted with the radio to take much notice of the signs that immediately precede the 'big silence'. Worse than not noticing the signs before the event, after it happened I consciously didn't do anything about it until I had finished my radio message. Only then did I make the necessary changes and switched on the booster pump for the engine to restart. It was after that I had to give myself a good telling-off: this had been the second big mistake in a single day through lack of care. The only good thing that came from that was that I did then realise I was pushing my luck too far. At least I was still able to learn from my mistakes.

A very misty view of Lisbon

Some 170nm (315km) from Lisbon I managed to establish two-way communications in VHF, admittedly far from perfect, but with the help of a Britannia flight all messages were transmitted both ways. Unfortunately, as I approached the city of my birth, the weather had deteriorated enough to prevent any view of the coast before actually crossing it. This was a great shame as I had particularly wanted to see the waterfront that I used to know so well and which is one of my favourite places in Portugal.

Lisbon Approach (the international airport) gave me vectors to join final for runway 36 of Cascais and then transferred me to the local tower just as I was about to cross the coast with a little over two miles to run. I had covered the distance in five hours and forty-nine minutes, GC distance of 755nm (1,398km) and I had just completed my crossing of the Atlantic. The actual flown distance was 838nm (1,552km) and I was back in continental Europe. The end of this adventure was starting to feel very close.

A marshal/courtesy driver was waiting for me to assist tying-down the aircraft and drive me to the terminal, where my brother João was waiting. This was, of course, more than an ordinary stop-over. First of all I didn't have to find a place in an anonymous hotel room because I had been invited by my brother to stay with him and his family and although my links with Portugal are now very tenuous, I still felt I was going back to my roots. This was further enhanced by the fact that João, a successful businessman in Lisbon, lives in what used to be our maternal grandfather's house, giving further pleasant links with my past and ancestry.

It was a long drive through the very heavy rush-hour traffic and we had lots of opportunity to chat and catch up on our not too frequent contacts. It was great to meet all his family again and the animated conversation went on until the early hours. Unfortunately not long after going to bed I started being violently sick to an extent that I began to suspect that there was something seriously wrong with my stomach. When 'events' followed their course down the digestive system, I knew I would survive and decided I must have had something that didn't agree with me. Maybe my insides could no longer cope with rich Portuguese food, especially after weeks of careful and frugal eating. Could it have been that it was a third example of dangerous complacency that day?

Those night events meant that by the morning I had had no sleep at all and I was feeling fragile and totally incapable of taxiing an aeroplane, let alone flying it! Black tea and dry toast helped a little and at least it gave us plenty of time to resume the previous night's chat.

At about midday I started to feel well enough to give it a go, so João drove me back to the airport, thankfully in a much-improved traffic situation as we didn't have to cope with the rush-hour hassle.

The weather system that I had skirted on my way here from the Azores was now blocking my direct route back home, so the alternative was to go the long way overland. As Cascais did not have customs facilities, I would be unable to go directly to the UK anyway and, as it was already 1.00 p.m., I decided to only go as far as La Rochelle in France. This precluded the requirement for customs as I would be staying within the Schengen Agreement airspace and would allow me to arrive there before sunset.[19] Hopefully it would be an easy, relaxed journey, despite most of Spain being covered by a thick layer of cloud.

João was allowed to come airside with me and it was amusing to see his expression when he saw how small G-RV was! Little brother very kindly paid for the landing fees and the fuel. *Obrigado João!*

Chapter 22
CASCAIS TO LA ROCHELLE

The way I had to carry out my power checks meant I was rather unpopular with the Cascais ATC. These checks, as the name implies, are designed to make sure that the engine and associated systems are functioning correctly. (It is obviously always better to find any engine problems on the ground.) And it is normal practice to carry them out in a place where the blast from the propeller is not going to damage other aircraft or generally inconvenience others. In this instance the problems started when the control tower was unable to direct me to a suitable place for the purpose, therefore forcing me to conduct them on the runway threshold. And as if that wasn't enough to rock the boat, I then had to refuse to compromise my safety by rushing such an important procedure, which obviously held up the use of the runway for the duration. I hope the instructor of the aircraft doing circuits who was unable to land understood my situation.

The departure clearance involved climbing on the 18 runway heading to the coast, then westwards alongside it, followed by a long loop to the right until north of Lisbon and then on a direct track to my first waypoint on the east of the country. As arranged, immediately after take-off I was transferred to Lisbon Approach, who straight away and unexpectedly changed my clearance by directing me into a left turn, effectively making me perform a wide turn over the sea just outside the River Tagus estuary. This was a navigational improvement saving time and distance, but it made me feel extremely uncomfortable as I had to remain under 1,000ft above the sea without the reassuring presence of my life jacket. Because I had been told to expect an overland clearance I wasn't wearing one for the first time in many thousands of miles of over-water flying and I found it most unsettling.

The weather hadn't changed much since the previous day and the visibility was poor. Once I was due south of Lisbon, ATC insisted on keeping me at the same level as a layer of clouds which wasn't good for sightseeing or in fact seeing anything at all. After pointing out that the VFR status of the flight was incompatible with their instruction, I was allowed to continue at a lower and more suitable level.

The visibility improved markedly once away from the coast and although I was still under a fairly low cloud base I could then watch Portugal pass under my wings, an exercise that unexpectedly felt rather strange. Although I was looking at a place I knew well, I just couldn't find a sense of belonging there within myself. There was a total absence of any emotional attachment, past or present, to the country in which I was born and I found this slightly disturbing. Nonetheless, the aerial perspective was good and I enjoyed the view.

As Portugal is less than 100nm (180km) wide west to east, I soon crossed the border into Spain and with it I left my identity dilemmas behind. Anticipating the high mountains in central Spain,

I climbed initially to FL085 with the co-operation of a very efficient and accommodating Spanish ATC. This help was most appreciated as further increases in height were required until at FL110

I finally had to accept there was no more room to outclimb the rising clouds in my oxygen-less status. Just before the city of Valladolid I had to descend to 1,500ft above ground to remain clear of cloud and ice, as the temperature away from direct sunlight had dropped to below freezing. Without sunshine and only mediocre visibility, the outlook was bleak but at least I was comfortably flying in compliance with VFR rules and away from the dreaded ice.

Towards the Pyrenees the terrain became fantastically spectacular with mountains topped by razor-sharp edges and deep valleys full of glorious colours, so I was treated to yet another great display of natural beauty. Although the relatively poor weather conditions and low clouds were forcing me to fly closer to the mountains than I would have chosen, it was not so close as to feel particularly uncomfortable and, on the plus side, I was treated to a much more dramatic view of the fabulous scenery.

Clearing the Spanish coast at San Sebastian, I left behind the weather system affecting the Iberian Peninsula and clipping the corner of the Bay of Biscay towards Biarritz I felt the warmth of the sun through the canopy and was once more enjoying blue skies. With only a little haze preventing the visibility from being perfect, the remainder of the flight over that very flat part of France was

pleasant and uneventful, despite my choice of a complex route around the many restricted military areas. The only time the flying became hard work was when I had to find the westerly-orientated runway at La Rochelle. The low setting sun and the haze exacerbated by the proximity of the coast pretty much reduced the forward visibility to zero. Good job the GPS doesn't have problems with that!

After using a particularly clever device to carry concrete blocks, I secured the aircraft to them for the night. As I knew that the tower personnel had already gone, I was a little concerned that the airfield appeared to be totally deserted with no visible way out of the

Top: The Tagus river near Spain
Above: Biarritz

tightly fenced-in airside part of the airport. After knocking at a few doors holding little hope of meeting anybody, I eventually found the only person still there, a fireman who saved the day by unlocking the terminal and letting me out.

Remembering that taxi drivers in France can usually be trusted to know where to find good food and decent hotels, I successfully relied on the driver who picked me up from the airport to take me to a comfortable hotel in town. The Hotel St Jean D'Arc indeed met this description and my room faced straight out to the splendid towers that guard the entrance to the old port. Even laying in bed I could see the west tower right in front one of the windows – it was a great setting for the last night of this adventure.

By the time I had settled into the room, my stomach appeared to have almost recovered from the Portuguese food episode and I thought it was sending me signs of hunger, or at least it must have been telling me that it was well enough to respond to the call of French cuisine. I had noticed upon my arrival that the street behind the hotel had a large number of restaurants, so I went out to answer that call.

As it is often the case in France, I easily found a small restaurant displaying all the right signs to comply with my rule of thumb for finding the perfect establishment; that is a restaurant heaving with local people as opposed to tourists and busy enough to have to wait for a table. I was cautious enough not to push my luck too far with anything exotic or elaborate, but the plain food I chose was still wonderful and the atmosphere inspiring. It was a great opportunity to look back on the last thirty-eight days and 23,000 nautical miles.

FRENCH MUSINGS

Coming out of the restaurant in a serene, happy and contemplative mood, I could see that night had descended over La Rochelle and the charming street towards the old port provided the ideal surroundings in which to reflect on the last few weeks. Immersed in my thoughts, I walked along the port with its yachts bobbing in the water and past the warmly-illuminated tower op posite that I had seen from my room, finally arriving at the seafront with the equally beautifully-lit city walls some way to my right.

So there I stood, enjoying the night in a silence that belied the proximity of the city, an eerie experience accentuated by the few people out there that were transformed into sketchy shapes by the backlighting effect of the fortified-wall illumination. The black velvety sky with its multitude of stars gave everything a glorious sense of serenity – inspiring places don't come much better than this.

While soaking up the atmosphere, I found myself idly watching a small red light out at sea slowly moving in my direction. In the stillness of the night the sound of an outboard engine preceded the shape of a small yacht with furled sails making its way towards the old port. As it passed by the place where I was standing, its occupants, barely discernible as silhouettes, suddenly became the embodiment of mystery to me. This arrival shrouded by the cloak of night generated an overwhelming curiosity as to what sort of adventures this small boat might have been returning from. It might have come from just around the corner, but it was equally possible that it was arriving from the most fantastic high sea adventure, maybe not unlike my own air adventure. As an outsider I could guess at their experiences, but I could not know their stories. Then it dawned on me that this was probably the way a lot of people had seen me.

However, although I could only guess at their journey, I certainly knew all about my own. What had I learnt from my odyssey around the world? It had all started out as the ultimate flying adventure, so it would have been reasonable to assume that it wouldn't ever quite match that expectation, let alone surpass it. However it had done so on both counts and now I wanted to analyse what I had discovered. Not just discoveries about the pilot within myself, but the discovery of situations, discovery of people, discovery of self.

One uncovering I could not have anticipated was a surprising facet of time. We know time as an objective dimension, such as hours, minutes and seconds which is the basis of all navigation and which, after all, had been a critical part of this journey. But there is also a subjective dimension of time relating to events within projects such as this. These events seem to have a life span and sequence of their own, all the way from the original idea to their culmination and as the climax of the whole project was about to happen, it gave the entire concept a much greater stature.

Such a course of events appear separate from normal life in the same way as sentences within brackets are separate from the main text. The contents of the brackets have an order of their own and they are linked by their own events and not by a conventional measure of time. One event precedes another and whether the clock has advanced one day or two years is not important, the sequence is what matters. I feel that this is an essential requisite for long and arduous projects such as this one. But the time outside the brackets is also reminding us of how long we can be separated from the essence of our lives (the real world?) and that is a clear sign that the contents of the brackets need the main body of the text for their very existence.

Away from these subjective and somewhat convoluted considerations, there was the discovery of a multitude of objective experiences. The experience of the expected was as fascinating as foreseen, no doubt helped by an obsessive attention to detail at the planning stage. The experience of the unexpected gave it a fantastic dimension.

Very high on the list of unexpected and unforgettable experiences, anxiety came top. Normally, anxiety is something I seldom experience, chiefly because it is a state of mind I detest. So on the few occasions when it has occurred in my life I have been able to dispel it with relative ease. However dilemmas over the accuracy of my fuel calculations, from a theoretical consideration to the very real possibility of ending up in the middle of a vast ocean, were to become a cause of a real anxiety that I couldn't dismiss. There were many other unforeseen occurrences, such as the experience of pushing myself through the overwhelming barriers of tiredness; the experience of seeing land after a long, difficult and sometimes terrifying ocean crossing; the experience of the generosity and hospitality of people of all creeds, colours and races ready to welcome me.

And the experience of seeing the world! The world with all its marvels, its beauty, its intricate natural secrets and its power, all of a magnitude clearly created at a much greater level than our own. The same world that has lured explorers to see and try to understand what lies beyond the horizon from time immemorial until this day and undoubtedly will continue to do so until the end of mankind.

Mankind, having taken root all over the world, from the most favourable conditions to the most difficult. Mankind, more often than not, solely concerned with their own little circle within their visible horizon or within their own inner limits – often a much more constrictive limitation. Whatever the conditions, it still is the same human being with all the qualities and failings of any other, the very same with whom I came into contact in so many varied places. Being able to visit so many 'little circles' of humanity in such a quick succession had been a unique privilege. It has been a privilege that has generated the most diverse feelings, from the intense repugnance of how low mankind can sink, to the discovery of selfless friendship that challenged my own pre-conceived prejudices. From seeing first-hand people living in harmony with nature and their environment, to the horrendous isolation of children exploited by distorted values. From witnessing those with suspicions generated by anything foreign to those who opened their arms unconditionally to this foreign traveller.

And then there was me, a foreign traveller that is no longer quite so unknown to himself, this foreign traveller who discovered how to be a little more understanding and ready to accept his own shortcomings, this foreign traveller that has understood a little more about pushing himself through the barriers of his own fears and limitations.

Chapter 23
HOMEWARD BOUND

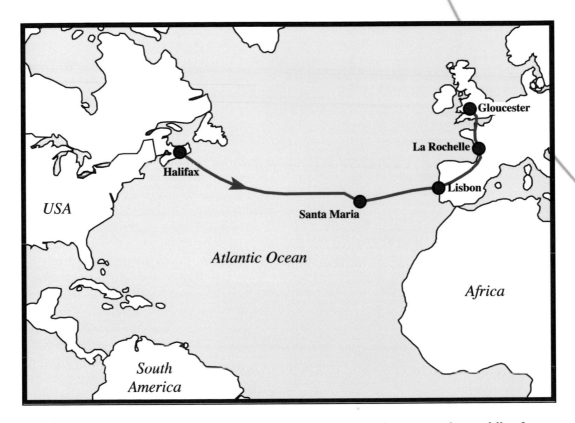

I woke up on the 8th April 2006 into a chaos of expectations, realisations and a muddle of emotions. This was it! Save for unforeseen disasters, today I was going to complete my circumnavigation and turn this dream of mine into reality.

Just as in all previous travelling days, my first task was to check the weather and I felt happy with what I found, despite a cold front slowly moving south across the English Channel. The likely bad weather of that front was not going to favour crossing through the Channel Islands' airspace as, in marginal conditions, it probably would have been difficult to comply with the necessary clearance required. So I decided it would be better to route to the east of the Cotentin (Cherbourg) Peninsula.

Being in complete awe of this final part of my circumnavigation was enough to disrupt my routine. Having to delay my departure to co-ordinate my arrival in Gloucester with Jill's website announcements completely confused it. After weeks of being obsessed with starting as early as possible, this waiting felt very strange and I found myself at a loss for something to do.

To help pass the time I went for a wander around the airport, confirming my belief that France is a particularly aviation-friendly place, with people kind and helpful to the passing pilot. On top of that it was also interesting to look around types of aircraft not so common elsewhere.

After having the mandatory cups of coffee and chatting with a few pilots, including a past 'Earthrounder' in a multi-crew TBM700, I felt compelled to buy fuel although I didn't actually need it. Despite the forecasted headwind, this was going to be a flight of less than three hours for which I already had plenty of fuel. However after going around for several weeks with huge amounts of fuel in the aircraft, taking off with what, by comparison, looked like empty tanks was just too uncomfortable for me to accept. As the overall weight wasn't going to be a problem, I gave up on logic, gave in to my niggling doubts and had the aircraft partially refuelled. While that was taking place I had to have a chuckle at the thought of the old aviation adage that the only time an aircraft has too much fuel on board is when it is on fire…

Once I finished my pre-flight checks, the cockpit looked as if it needed a good tidying up and that's when the immersion suit in the luggage compartment caught my eye. Although I had crossed the channel many times before without an immersion suit, seeing it at the bottom of the luggage bay made me wonder if it was a good idea to leave it there, as I no longer could forget my preoccupation with ditching survival. On top of these life-extending considerations, I knew that if the worst came to the worst, the possibility of the wreckage of the aeroplane being found with the immersion suit still in the back and my body perished through hypothermia, was simply too ludicrous to contemplate. I could just imagine the lounge experts, upon reading the accident report, pronouncing the verdict of, 'oh, what a prat', throughout the country's aero clubs! As this was not an epitaph of choice, I wriggled myself into the suit for one last time.

After leaving La Rochelle, my route went overhead Nantes airport, passed close to Rennes and crossed the coast just to the east of the Cotentin Peninsula. With only a few miles to go to the French coast, I met the cold front anticipated in the forecast, but as the terrain was low and

flat I was able to cross it without undue drama, despite low clouds, lots of rain and a low icing level. Just about that time Deauville ATC asked the origin and destination of the flight and I was tempted to state the obvious: Gloucester to Gloucester via the world, but I managed to refrain from flippant comments – just!

Soon after coasting out from France I had to deal with a further line of low cloud and rain, but then the weather improved all the way to the English coast and I crossed the shoreline by Selsley Bill in glorious sunshine.

Opposite: The first sighting of England!
Above: Arrival at Gloucester *(Photograph by David Haines)*

The elation of actually overflying the English countryside once again was indescribable. Being back home was simply glorious and it even appeared as if the weather had put on a special effort to welcome me back. In fact everything felt special, great, unique, fantastic and every possible positive superlative that exists in all the languages I know.

The magnificent weather wasn't just confined to the coast, it remained fabulous all the way to Gloucester and even though the sprinkling of cumulus clouds resulted in a somewhat choppy ride, it was certainly not enough to impair the enjoyment of overflying the beautiful green English countryside once again.

Arriving at the Cotswold escarpment just to the east of Cheltenham I was directed to an unusual left base for runway 27, which was very welcome as this was also the shortest way in. On a very short final, almost at the threshold of the runway, a glance over to my left revealed Jill surrounded by an amazing crowd waiting for me in the viewing area, a fantastic and unexpected sight.

Just prior to flaring for the landing and therefore only a few feet above the runway, the familiar friendly voice of a fellow pilot came over the radio congratulating me for the successful completion of my round the world flight. This was music to my ears, but I had to make a point of declining the compliment as I felt I would have been pushing my luck to accept it before I had actually finished. The landing itself was carried out as normal, as was the vacating of the runway. I suppose I was sufficiently focused and in plenty of flying practice to put all spurious thoughts to one side and carry on with the task in hand.

Once I was directed to the Cotswold Aero Club apron, I had a choice of taxiways to make my way there and decided to take taxiway 'H', which happens to be out of view of most people and I am glad I chose it because that was when the most intensely emotional moment of the whole flight took place. The sudden relaxation after the last part of the flight brought me face to face with the highest and lowest avalanche of emotions of the whole adventure. It was the highest point

Top: Back home! *(Photograph by David Haines)*
Middle: The cheering crowd *(Photograph by Ian Leigh)*
Bottom: The author with his wife Jill, and a bottle of
   champagne *(Photograph by Richard Crosby)*

because I had done it, I had achieved my goal and no matter what else could possibly happen, nobody could take it away from me. Even if the aircraft completely disintegrated underneath me, I had done it and I was back home!

On the other hand being back home meant that this was it, there was no more adventure to be lived. It was over and that was obviously also the lowest point. This clash of emotions seriously messed me up and I found myself both uncontrollably laughing and in an equally chaotic manner crying my eyes out. For a while I simply couldn't control it. Towards the end of the taxiway I spotted my friend Ralph Vincent and rapidly closing on him was the push I needed to compose myself sufficiently to wave at him in a reasonably decorous manner.

Taxiing into the apron, I was taken aback by the crowd of people surging from the gate towards the aircraft. This was both amazing and scary as I had visions of masses of people turning into minced meat by walking into the turning propeller! However, young Ashley did his marshalling job well and I stopped the engine without any ghastly mishaps.

Jill, who I could see at the front of the crowd, closely beat the TV camera crew in the race to the aeroplane. It was indescribably good to be able hold her again, no matter what else was going on. As for the TV camera, if they wanted to record it from what felt like inches away, they could do what they like, that moment was too good to worry about who was looking.

The whole thing was just a dream! Jill, Natalie, Eva, Matthew, Helen, Derek, Ian, friends, acquaintances, people I had no idea who they were, champagne… Thanks all, thank you Jill!

Epilogue
REFLECTIONS

When in November 2000 I declared I was going to fly solo around the world, I really had no idea what I was letting myself in for. In fact, reality didn't kick in until quite a lot later, so this stage of events could have been called the 'fairy-tale' stage – I only had a dream to do what only a handful of pilots had ever done, but little else.

Nonetheless, I was determined to carry out that dream and that determination was going to be the one single element that made sure the project came into fruition, despite the numerous obstacles and difficulties I found along the way. In 2000 I had a vague idea of how important that determination was going to be, but very soon it really became obvious just how essential it was; so much so that I found myself on a parallel mission to demonstrate to the world that aspirations and dreams, everybody's, are within reach.

From a very early stage I felt compelled to show that being rich or having access to substantial resources were not essential conditions to successfully completing such a monumental task. It was not easy: it required huge amounts of perseverance and the acceptance of all manner of risks. I think I demonstrated beyond doubt however that it can be done, despite severe limitations of finance, contacts and expertise. The reason for this is disarmingly simple: if we want something badly enough, the determination to get it will always ensure that we find ways around whatever obstacles come our way. However it is imperative to desperately want to achieve our goal.

I discovered that the most difficult hurdles are those from within and that they are invariably related to fear of pushing our own limits. This is particularly unfortunate as I firmly believe that we are capable of much more than our everyday lives allow and if we don't push those limits we will never realise our full potential. Fear of public failure is also a major problem, particularly failure in full view of our peers. Of course, to try to surmount these obstacles and the more obvious external ones, involves taking risks and there is no guarantee of success at any individual point. The important thing is that after any and every failure we remember that the way forward is to get up and get on with the next hurdle on our chosen path.

Throughout my adventure there were many failures: to secure finance; to overcome bureaucracy; of mechanical systems; and of self-confidence. It was only through determination that an alternative was always found. Although instant gratification was out of the question, the eventual sense of achievement more than compensated for that.

Perseverance certainly had to be strong as it was a solid slog all the way to the end of February 2006, when the actual journey started and then everything changed. It had been a long and difficult path, but it was behind me. Not only had I reached the next and final stage, but I was happy that all aspects of my preparation were as thorough as they could have been and I could allow myself to concentrate on the job in hand.

The job had been the light at the end of the tunnel all that time, a sort of aviator's nirvana where I could dedicate all my time, energies and resources to flying the ultimate flight. This required much more than the routine stuff that constitutes the great majority of flying by the average private pilot, of which of course I was one.

Expanding the envelope of my flying experience was one of the major objectives of this adventure and I found it as fulfilling as I had anticipated. Looking back over the many instances when my piloting was fully extended it all now seems that most of it was inevitable and foreseeable. But it wasn't then and being such a fantastic part of this adventure, it is worth looking at the highlights.

Navigation was one of them. Navigational considerations left much less room for error than ever before and the huge distances over the seas, obviously devoid of visible marker features, were a big challenge. Of course, I was using GPS as my primary navigational aid, but my backup method of pencil, paper and brain had to be able to take over if the unlikely, but entirely possible, GPS failure took place. As this could have occurred at any time this task was absolutely critical – in the middle of an ocean there are no handy fields to carry out a precautionary landing and sort out the finer details of the route, or of anything else for that matter!

Fuel management was also an obvious and important consideration, not only to ensure that I could reach my destinations, but also to distribute the huge weight of fuel I was carrying, which was over three times the normal quantity. This distribution not only affected the lateral balance but also the position fore and aft of the centre of gravity of the aircraft with its critical influence on performance. Closely related to fuel management was the handling of the engine and the monitoring of all the aircraft systems in order to fly at optimum efficiency and spot any unwanted trends before they developed into problems.

As well as these on-board considerations, there were the communications with the outside world, often in the form of HF radio position reports. I also had to contend with weather systems of a much greater magnitude than I had ever had to deal with, in fact which on more than one occasion threatened to prematurely finish the journey and possibly me. Similarly, this latter grim possibility could well have happened if I'd allowed my fatigue to get out of hand. Ensuring that I could cope with tiredness and sleep deprivation in a long series of flights, some exceeding fifteen non-stop hours, was a demanding and important part of this adventure.

Despite having placed my hopes on a very high pedestal, all these aspects of flying fully satisfied my expectations. But, amazingly, it was even better than that. Two unforeseen factors made this adventure surpass all I had anticipated.

The first factor came from the people I met.

As this was purely a solo flight without any supporting team of any kind, before the journey started I had never seen the 'people factor' as relevant. But, of course, at the end of every flying day I found myself in a completely new environment, often in a new country and sometimes in a new continent. And in all of these places I met all sorts of people, not only at a necessary and operational level, but also in an everyday context. Crucially, the manner in which I met so many different people was essential to the quality of my experience. This was due to the way I travelled: I was totally on my own, without a cushion or barrier between me and the people I met – not a cruise ship organisation, not a tour operator, not a travel agency rep, not even airline staff, just me on my own and the people of the world's continents.

I thus had the opportunity to mix with people from the most diverse backgrounds and ethnic origins in their own surroundings. In turn, this freedom of communication gave me an insight into the human condition, which although I hadn't expected it, helped me to understand a little more about mankind, making the whole experience unforgettable.

That human experience was as varied as the world is wide, it ranged from the bad to the good, from the cool and polite to the enthusiastically effusive, from the officious to the informal, from the greedy to the generous. All these human traits had the common element of being expressions of mankind, the very same that has spread itself all over the world. Although man has populated all corners of the earth and even our physical appearance has accordingly adapted itself, we are still spectacularly similar deep down. In order to claim our little cave/field/company/country we have built barriers and borders – and once we had found a better cave than our neighbours, then we call the ones inside 'us' and the ones outside 'them'.

While I was travelling around the world, it often occurred to me that many of the world's woes could be addressed if large numbers of the world's population travelled in this same manner. As such we could all see what goes on in other people's backyards and that 'them' are really just part of 'us', undoubtedly leading to a much better and safer planet.

However, having said that there were no barriers between me and the people of the world, I was omitting one type that is not visible but is nonetheless very real – and that relates to one's own prejudices when confronted with different customs and appearances. That these prejudices can be aggravated by logistical and other practical considerations only makes matters worse and there are times when it requires a certain amount of positive effort to isolate our own problems from those surrounding us. As to the arrogance of expecting the world to follow our own domestic habits, I feel it just has no place within civilised behaviour and I believe that it is always good to remember that we are guests in somebody else's country and need to act accordingly.

The second unexpected bonus of this journey came from nature itself.

Pilots of small aircraft are well aware of the power of nature, as lack of harmony with our surroundings sooner or later ends in tears, but this flight brought a new facet to that awareness.

Being alone for hours on end and thousands of miles at a time, while flying through the most varied natural conditions, gives an intimacy with nature that we are seldom lucky enough to experience in our modern world.

First of all, by simply having so much time without the distraction of the hustle and bustle of twenty-first century everyday life, the wonders of what I saw outside inspired me into meditation. And it was not just what I saw but also what I felt in terms of movement, temperature, humidity and smells that held me in intimate contact with nature. I understand that long distance solo sailors share similar experiences, but I think I had the edge with my capability of flying over land as well as sea, to say nothing of speed!

But what really is awesome is nature itself. The power of the elements in all its manifestations, such as how some mountains have been created by volcanic eruptions, how others were sculptured by water and wind and the oceans, occupying the largest part of the planet's surface, hide a whole life system in conditions that remains out of our reach, despite our technology. These are all expressions of nature that we all know about, but actually being in such a fantastic position with little outside interference is an enormous privilege that offers an unparalleled and heightened appreciation. Seeing, for instance, the path of a tsunami that moved an ocean in a fraction of the time that my aeroplane took to overfly a corner of it, or simply witnessing the power of towering clouds that can destroy any aeroplane that strays into its internal currents is both a humbling and enlightening experience.

Despite spectacular developments in science and industry, the efforts of mankind appear pathetic when compared with nature's work. This is not limited to the great natural cataclysms – simply contemplating everyday events such as tidal movements lifting whole oceans is just mind blowing. From a more personal viewpoint, the simple experience of travelling hundreds and hundreds of miles without seeing another human being is a fantastic reality check. With the natural forces being so far above our own capability, mankind may well be seen as an irrelevant and miniscule passenger.

From these considerations to the big 'why' and 'how' and 'who' creates and controls it is only a short hop – and those are questions that just have to be asked, even if we are not in a position to answer them. Maybe merely asking is a step towards understanding.

Although the big questions may well have to remain unsolved, there was a particular and personal one I did manage to answer. This related to fear, how to deal with it and the notion of courage. In my early formative years I was led to believe that simply experiencing fear was a sign of weakness and flawed character. The doubt hence seeded in my subconscious regarding the veracity of such a statement and my own experience of fear remained with me and, despite the passing of time, always left an unpleasant disquietedness. As a result of having gone through the most difficult and intense moments of this adventure, I now have my own definition of courage as the ability to win the fight over our own fears, not over the outside difficulties or threats. I also learnt that total absence of fear is either pathological or comes in a bottle.

Faced with these discoveries and achievements, it is very easy to forget where I started and the messages I wanted to take to the world that can be overshadowed by all that excitement. So it is time to remember that the aircraft was called SLAVKA for a reason. Slavka was a good friend that lost her war against cancer soon after I had been lucky enough to have won my own battle against the same disease. I hope to have successfully carried the message around the world that despite being a lethal enemy that affects as much as one in three persons, cancer can be overcome. I had hoped that Cancer Research UK would have showed more enthusiasm and support for the project so they could have benefited more from this adventure than the modest amounts I raised. That they did not was their decision.

With the more serious side of the event in mind and several months after my return it was safe to assume that all that excitement was well behind me. Wrong again! There was still one huge surprise to come. In April 2007 I had the honour of being awarded the most prestigious of all British trophies in aviation, the Britannia Trophy. This trophy is awarded to 'the British aviator or aviators accomplishing the most meritorious performance in aviation during the preceding year', and the list of it recipients encompasses some of the most famous names in British aviation since 1913. Seeing my own name joining the list of those that had held it before me certainly was a humbling experience. I am hugely grateful to the PFA for nominating me and the Royal Aero Club for choosing me, particularly as they are not obliged to award this trophy every year. That I actually received this most prestigious of awards from the president of the Royal Aero Club, HRH The Duke of York, made the occasion absolutely perfect.

But now that the dust has settled and my head isn't quite so much in the clouds, looking back over the years dedicated to this adventure I see again aspects of the human element that shines bright in my collection of memories. I am referring here to the help I was given in an unassuming and generous manner, such as those that helped me with the preparation work, both with an actual hands-on physical presence and those that so kindly sponsored my efforts. I will forever be indebted to all of you.

Opposite: Receiving the Britannia Trophy from HRH The Duke of York *(Copyright Belgrave & Portman Photography Ltd)*
Above: With Jill and Britannia *(Photograph by Matthew Paull)*

However, my admiration and gratitude goes above all to the real hero of this adventure, Jill, my dear, beautiful and patient wife, whose quiet generosity and fantastic ability to counterweigh my excesses with crystal clear practicality made it all possible and to whom I dedicate this narrative.

Appendix A
G-GDRV SPECIFICATION

G-GDRV is a Van's RV-6, an American kit aeroplane that was built in 1993 by an amateur in Canada.

Van's, complete with apostrophe, is the name of the most prolific ever range of kit-built aircraft. It is so-called because Richard VanGrunsven (Van for short) is the man behind it all – so, with typical American logic, his designs are called Van's. Straight from his name, we also have the individual type designators all starting with RV, the initials of the man himself.

The RV-6, the company's first side-by-side two-seater aircraft, is the most numerous of the family with over 2,400 examples flying worldwide. Its high performance and exemplary manoeuvrability ensure this popularity, despite a laborious building schedule.

With a 160 horsepower engine the performance figures for the basic aircraft were:

Top speed	202mph
Stall speed	50mph
Fast cruise @ 8,000'	190mph
Take-off distance (solo)	91 metres
Landing distance (solo)	91 metres
Rate of climb (solo)	1,900 feet/minute
Ceiling	18,000 feet
Range, fast cruise	775 statue miles

The main dimensions were:

Span	23ft
Length	20ft 2in
Height	5ft 3in
Wing area	110sq ft
Empty weight	965lbs
Gross weight	1,600lbs
Engine	150-180hp
Propeller	fixed pitch or C/S
Fuel capacity	38 US gal

Significant changes from standard relating to the 'Chasing the Morning Sun' configuration:

Top speed (max. weight)	190mph
Stall speed (max. weight)	75mph
Normal cruise speed	160mph (refer to text)

Take-off distance (max. weight)	400 metres
Rate of climb (max. weight)	700 feet/minute
Ceiling (calculated)	15,000 feet
Range	2,760 statue miles
Empty weight	1,360lbs
Maximum weight	2,000lbs
Maximum landing weight	1,800lbs
Fuel capacity	120 US gal

For 'Chasing the Morning Sun' the instrumentation was expanded beyond the basic setup.

The panel instrumentation consisted of:

• Full '6 pack' flight instruments (air speed indicator, attitude indicator, altimeter, turn co-ordinator, direction indicator, vertical speed indicator)
• Digital 'Rocky Mountains' engine monitor.
• Magnetic compass.
• Nav/Com 'Bendix-King' KX155 VHF radio with VOR/Glide indicator.
• 'Bendix-King' KT76A transponder with 'AmeriKing' altitude encoder
• 'Bendix-King' Skymap IIIC moving map GPS.
• Dual fuel gauges to monitor inside and outside fuel tanks.
• Intercom to talk to myself.
• Modified 'Icom' IC-703 HF radio set.
• 'TruTrak' auto-pilot with altitude hold.
• Heated pitot tube.
• Dimmable panel and interior illumination by post 'P' lights and 2 directional cockpit lights.

Power plant:

• Standard 160hp Lycoming engine freshly rebuilt with cylinder head and exhaust gas temperature transducers from engine monitor to all cylinders.
• Standard fixed-pitch Sensenich propeller for optimum cruise speed.
Air filter box with automatic trap door to minimise impact icing.

Fuel system:

• Standard system complemented by 'Jon Johanson' wingtip tanks of 34lt capacity each.
• Two cockpit tanks consisting of a 160lt seat tank and a 80lt passenger footwell tank.
• Total capacity 452 litres.
• Fuel system designed by Frazer-Nash Ltd. Fuel tanks directly selected via an Andair four-way fuel selector. Fuel flow transducer for engine monitor.

Aerodynamics and various:

Late specification undercarriage fairings installed to maximise wheel coverage. All gaps sealed as per glider practice. Flaps and ailerons rigged to reduce drag to a minimum. Pilot relief tube.

Appendix B
FLYING LOG BOOK

DATE UTC	FROM	TO	FLIGHT TIME hh-mm	GC DISTANCE NM	DISTANCE KM	SPEED Knots Km/hour
February 28th	Gloucester EGBJ	Luqa, Malta LMML	7-59	1,196	2,213	149.9kt 277.3kmh
March 1st	Luqa	Luxor, Egypt HELX	7-40	1,118	2,070	145.8kt 270kmh
March 2nd	Luxor	Muscat, Oman OOMS	9-23	1,399	2,589	149.1kt 275.9kmh
March 4th	Muscat	Colombo, Sri Lanka VCBI	11-52	1,588	2,939	133.8kt 247.7kmh
March 5th	Colombo	Penang, Malaysia WMKP	10-10	1,222	2,261	120.2kt 222.4kmh
March 6th	Penang	Manila, Philippines RPLL	10-27	1,344	2,487	128.6kt 238kmh
March 8th/9th	Manila	Guam, Mariana Islands PGUM	10-06	1,386	2,565	137.2kt 253.9kmh
March 10th/11th	Guam	Bonriki, Kiribati NGTA	14-21	1,834	3,394	127.8kt 236.5kmh
March 13th/14th	Bonriki	Honolulu, Hawaii PHNL	16-18	2,074	3,837	127.2kt 235.4kmh
March 17th/18th	Honolulu	Hilo, Hawaii PHTO	1-40	187	348	112.2kt 208.8kmh

DATE UTC	FROM	TO	FLIGHT TIME hh-mm	GC DISTANCE NM	DISTANCE KM	SPEED Knots Km/hour
March 21st	Hilo	Hilo	0-54	Sightseeing	Sightseeing	-
March 22nd	Hilo	San Jose, California KSJC	15-28	2,026	3,750	131kt 242.5kmh
March 23rd/24th	San Jose	Apple Valley, California KAPV	2-12	285	528	129.5kt 240kmh
March 24th	Apple Valley	Abilene, Texas KABI	6-27	885	1,637	137.2kt 253.8kmh
March 26th	Abilene	Savannah, Georgia KSAV	6-18	937	1,733	148.7kt 275.1kmh
March 27th	Savannah	Bangor, Maine KBGR	7-06	956	1,769	134.6kt 249.2kmh
March 29th	Bangor	Halifax, Nova Scotia, Canada CYHZ	1-41	226	419	134.3kt 248.9kmh
April 4th	Halifax	Santa Maria, Azores LPAZ	12-46	1,784	3,302	140.11kt 259.49kmh
April 6th	Santa Maria	Cascais, Portugal LPCS	5-49	756	1,398	130.68kt 242.02kmh
April 7th	Cascais	La Rochelle, France LFBH	4-46	575	1,063	120.6kt 223kmh
April 8th	La Rochelle	Gloucester UK EGBJ	2-50	345	639	121.8kt 225.5kmh

Appendix C
RECORDS

All my records were in compliance with the FAI Sub-Class C-1b: Landplanes with a take-off weight of between 500 and 1000kgs.

In addition to successfully circumnavigating the globe, I also obtained the following records:

- British National Speed Record for Circumnavigation

and

- Six World Records for Speed over a Recognised Course:

  Gloucester to Luqa, Malta (277.35 kmh)

  Muscat, Oman to Colombo, Sri Lanka (247.68 kmh)

  Hilo, Hawaii to San Jose, California (242.47 kmh)

  Halifax, Nova Scotia to Santa Maria, Azores (259.49 kmh)

  Halifax, Nova Scotia to Cascais, Portugal (76.35 kmh)

  Santa Maria Azores to Cascais, Portugal (242.02 kmh)

Appendix D
STATISTICS

Total distance flown	23,527 nautical miles	43,533km
Total flying hours	165h 19mins	
Average distance per flying day	1,106nm	2,046km
Average flying speed	142kt	263kmh
Longest leg	2,074nm	3,837km
Distance flown over the sea	15,684nm	29,022km

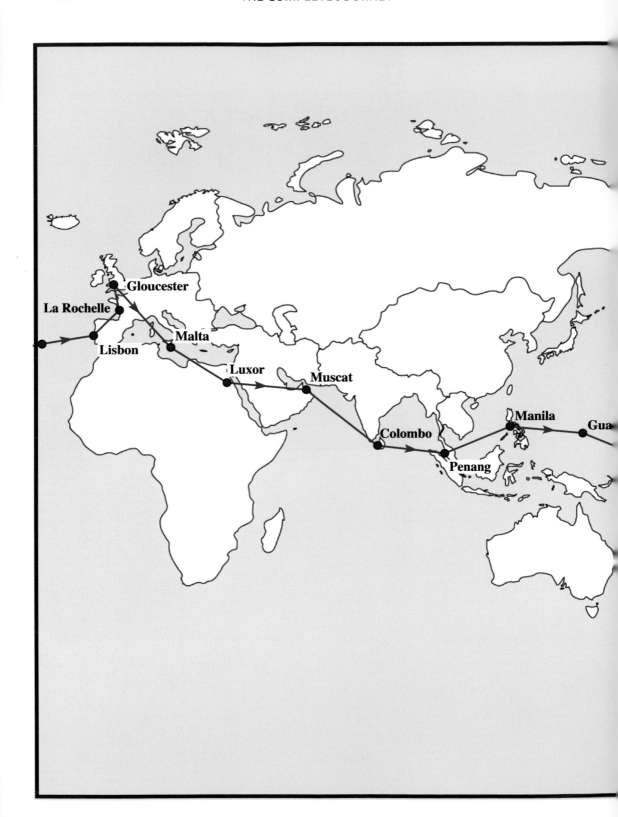

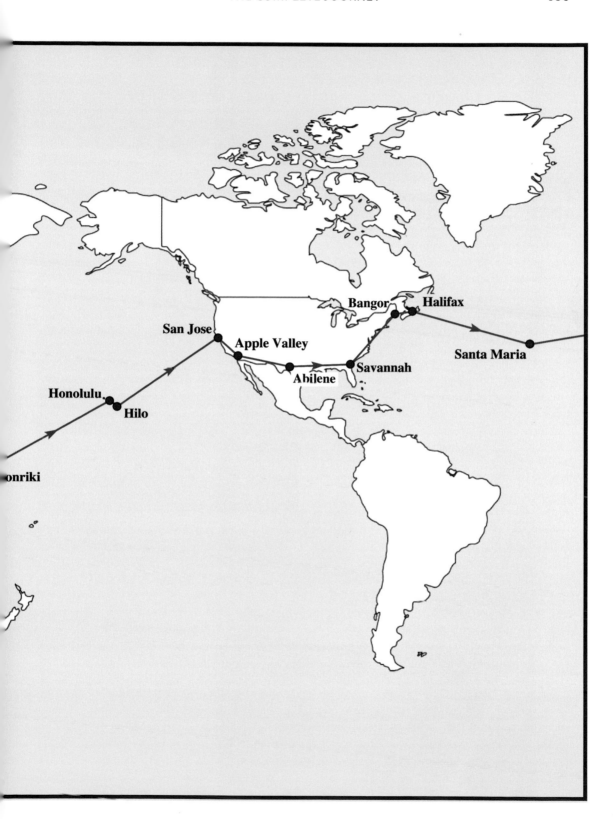

[1] Latitude is the angular distance on a meridian from the equator. A meridian is a circle passing through the geographical poles.

[2] The great circle path between A and B is represented by the intersection of the earth surface by a plane passing through both A, B and the centre of the Earth.

[3] All parts and systems in a certified aircraft are required to have a documented history from raw materials to completed item, as well as a trace of supply line to comply with provenance standards.

[4] A stall occurs when the airflow over the wing breaks down and the wing loses most of its lift, and effectively stops flying. There is no relation to an engine stoppage, as understood in a motoring context.

[5] An engine is considered time expired when it has reached its time between overhauls (TBO). It may be used after this time for private use and under specific conditions.

[6] 9G signifies an acceleration of nine times the magnitude of the acceleration of gravity.

[7] Wash-in is the increase of the angle of incidence of the wing from the root to the tip, resulting in a greater angle of attack at the tip, therefore causing the tip to stall before the rest of the wing.

[8] VOR (very high frequency omni-directional radio range) is a radio navigation aid.

[9] The Earthrounders are the group of pilots that have circumnavigated the globe in a light aircraft and form a loose voluntary association to share ideas and information.

[10] The static system provides certain instruments and the auto-pilot with a sensing point for the ambient pressure unaffected by dynamic pressure due to speed.

[11] As a further illustration of this point, some fifty years ago there was a Canadian study about the behaviour of pilots without an instrument rating flying a high-performance aeroplane and entering cloud at low level. They concluded that their life expectancy in those conditions would have been a mere sixty seconds!

[12] Speed, contrary to popular belief, is not so much a factor of engine power but it is mainly dependant on the pitch attitude of the aircraft – gravity is more powerful (and reliable) than horse power!

[13] A ground loop is a violent, often damaging, 180° turn on the ground, without any relationship to the 'loop' aerobatic manoeuvre.

[14] Usually the first letter of an aircraft registration refers to its nationality. G is for Great Britain, N for USA. US registrations can have the N followed by anything between one and four digits before one or two letters. Civilian British registrations always have the G followed by four letters.

[15] Burt Rutan designed, amongst others, Voyager, Virgin Global Flyer and Spaceship One, the first privately-funded craft to go into space.

[16] Canadian-registered aircraft have a C as their first letter, as in fact the RV did when it was built in Canada as C-GDRV, as opposed to its current British registration of G-GDRV.

[17] An airworthiness directive is a notification to owners and operators of certified aircraft from the manufacturers that there is a known fault with the aircraft which must be corrected.

[18] The white arc of the air speed indicator (ASI) denotes the speed range where flaps can be used.

[19] The European countries complying with this agreement ensure full freedom of movement between them with no internal borders. The UK (and Denmark) is outside this area and requires customs and immigration checks. This was relevant to my flight as the airport in Portugal where I was did not have facilities to clear me to go outside the Schengen area.

INDEX